THE
DON CHERRY
STORY

CINDY CHERRY

Tellwell Talent
www.tellwell.ca

ISBN
978-1-77941-399-4 (Hardcover)
978-1-77941-398-7 (Paperback)
978-1-77941-400-7 (eBook)

TABLE OF CONTENTS

PREFACE

As of November 9, 2019, Coach's Corner was no more after thirty-seven years. It took on the test of time, with Dad giving his take on the world of hockey and much more. Canada has dramatically changed throughout those years. Some may say for the better, others not so much. One thing is true: I, Cindy Cherry, witnessed it all from a particular point of view, one of a family member. It has been mentioned to me many times that I should write a book. I always shrugged it off, thinking an offspring writing a book about a family's intimate tales may appear biased or, worse, like a money grab by someone with an axe to grind.

Fortunately—or unfortunately—I have a Google Alert set for my dad. I never want to miss a thing, whether good or bad. One day some no-name columnist gave their article a headline that read NO MORE CHERRY in red type, followed by, "League gets it right by distancing themselves from Don Cherry." The writer was referring to the Western Hockey League's 2017–2020 campaign to promote organ transplants in Canada, titled "The WHL Suits Up with Don Cherry to Promote Organ Donation." In the first two years of this drive they raised close to half a million dollars by headlining Dad.

Then came the last year of the promotion, after the Poppygate saga in November 2019, when they chose to remove his name from the title of the campaign. This is what the reporter was agreeing with in his column. This Google Alert was the straw that broke the camel's back, and I decided I'd had enough. A lot was written around that time and it was analyzed to death, with everyone chirping in. The family kept quiet, taking the slings and arrows. Even Dad, though it would have been easy to lash out, didn't respond. It is now time to incorporate that saga into this book.

So much has been written about Dad, but none of it has captured the true Don Cherry. These writers have put spins on his character, but I thought it was time to *really* explain him, to give the big picture. A lot of people think they know him; trust me, most don't. It's amazing how many people think they do, but they don't have a clue what he is really thinking.

So here it is, for all of you who enjoyed watching Coach's Corner. It's even for the ones who watched to get angry at him—you still watched. You enjoyed that family time. It was a tradition in so many homes. It was like he was talking to you. Many people have told me that. He said things many of you were thinking but were too afraid to say. In the end he paid the price for that. The bigwigs in their ivory towers finally had the ammo they needed to rid themselves of a controversial figure. Canada was changing, has changed. In the years to come, if someone who doesn't know hockey asks why this guy was fired for something he had done for so long, the basic answer will be, well, he wanted more people to wear poppies for Remembrance Day and a lot of people took offence, so a big corporation relieved him of his post on that very day: November 11, 2019.

Please enjoy this book. Though there are a lot of hockey references in it, I have tried to write it not as a sports book, but as the life story of a man so many Canadians came to know. They even voted him number 7 in a public poll by CBC in 2004 to decide who was the greatest Canadian of all time.

But I already knew that.

PART 1
POPPYGATE AND OTHER CONTROVERSIES

CHAPTER 1
POPPYGATE

O n November 9, 2019, during the first intermission of Hockey Night in Canada (HNiC)—a Toronto Maple Leafs home game against the Philadelphia Flyers—Coach's Corner was about to come on. The tradition was to acknowledge that Remembrance Day was coming up, by doing so Dad would end the broadcast by showing a clip of him visiting the Canadian National Vimy Memorial in Pas-de-Calais, France, in 2007.[1]

Before the clip was shown Dad proceeded to go off script, addressing "those people", who chose not to buy a poppy pin in support of the Royal Canadian Legion. At the end of this broadcast, I wondered if he would receive mild backlash about it, never dreaming I had just watched the final

---

[1]   There is an interesting side story to this trip, which involved CBC's documentary series, *Who do You Think You Are?* Dad and my brother Tim visited this memorial in France, which commemorated the more than 11,000 Canadian soldiers killed there, many of whom died in the Battle of Vimy Ridge in 1917. There was not one person there visiting until a tour bus filled with Canadians showed up. You can only imagine the surprise and glee for them to meet Don Cherry so far away from Canada. They stayed another hour, signing autographs, and, needless to say, pictures were taken. The guide, who had no idea whom this celebrity was, asked Tim, "What is your dad known for in Canada?" Tim humbly said, "Well, he is a sports commentator." The gentleman then asked, "Is he on every day, since everyone knows him?" "No," Tim explained. "He's only on once per week." "Does he talk about the entire game?" My brother had to explain that he is only on once a week for about six minutes, to which the guy says, "That must be a helluva six minutes."

Coach's Corner. He told me long afterwards that, after that speech, he looked at co-host Ron MacLean and said, "We may be hearing about that one." Ron just looked at him inquisitively, indicating that Ron might not have been listening as intently as Dad thought. However, he was bobbing his head in agreement throughout the dialogue, gave Dad the thumbs-up at the end, and said, "Love you for it." In fairness to Ron, it is incredible how he can concentrate when the producers are talking in his ear while Coach's Corner is going on. Plus, I believe HNiC repeated this Coach's Corner for both their Central Canadian viewers. How bad could they have felt it was if they rebroadcasted it?

Throughout the years of the producers talking to Ron during Coach's Corner, none came on as strong as when the subject came up about the Iraq War in 2003. Dad started to give his opinion about the Canadian government not supporting the U.S. military when they were attacking the regime of Saddam Hussein in Iraq during the Gulf War in the nineties. Dad said you could hear them screaming in Ron's ear to get off this topic, with Ron replying, on air, "No, no, we're not moving on. Don't worry about it." Dad knew this was a touchy topic to be discussing and that nothing good could come from it. Liberal-thinking Ron kept pushing Dad to justify his support of the U.S. Dad kept using the scenario of, "If you are in a bar and your friend gets into a fight, would you not support him?" I believe Ron's take was, "Not if he was in the wrong," while Dad's philosophy is, "No matter what, you support your buddy."

Hmm . . . this philosophy sounds familiar now that I am writing it.

Needless to say, they really went at it for that Coach's Corner. Dad told me that, at the end, they looked at each other in silence. It was so controversial that I don't think CBC even put it on their website afterwards—even if you google it, it's nowhere to be found. That Monday, Ruth-Ellen Soles, a spokesperson for CBC, addressed it by saying, "CBC does not feel HNiC is the appropriate place for discussion on the war in Iraq." CBC ombudsman (the person responsible for investigating complaints against the company) David Bazay said he received a "handful of complaints." I believe the CBC's Sports' executive director at the time, did talk to Dad and Ron about it that Monday; however, they continued together for another fifteen years. Knowing that he had weathered the storm after that tirade (plus other controversial subjects, such as, "It's mostly French guys that wear visors," "It's always a woman yapping at the game that gets hit with the puck," etc.), I figured *no worries*. Since I was in Ottawa at a trade show for the weekend, my biggest concern was remembering to wear a poppy the next day at my booth.

Not being a big social media hound, when I walked into the show the next morning everyone came running, asking me if I had heard all the hoopla about Dad. I chuckled, never realizing it was such a big deal, and made sure I had a poppy on. Even at the show, most people mentioning it to me said he was correct in what he was saying. My friend Leanne said that, while she was watching, she turned to her friend and said, "I guess he's talking about me—I forgot to get a poppy!" This to me proved that if people weren't wearing one they would either take offence or feel guilty, which motivated them to go out and get one, which was the point.

After a long day at the show tearing down the booth and driving back to Toronto, I got a call from my brother Tim. Ironically, he and his wife were down in New York City celebrating Veterans' Day by wearing a poppy and visiting the Ground Zero reflecting pools, with the names of the victims of 9/11 etched around them. They found the name of Garnet Ace Bailey, a one-time Boston Bruin and a scout for the LA Kings who had been killed in the plane that hit the south tower. When they found his name, they placed their poppies on it. Ace never played for Dad but Tim knew him, as he once came over to our house in North Andover, Massachusetts.

He told me that, upon his arrival in NYC, he was met with a call from Sportsnet. But little did Tim know, Rogers Sports & Media, had already visited Dad at his house that Sunday morning. It was there that they gave him their demands, which were more than just saying sorry. I'm sure Dad's parting words to them were, "You gotta do what you gotta do."

They asked Tim to try to talk Dad into saying he was sorry. Tim, who didn't know of the other stipulations, said that there was no way Dad was going to read a prewritten PR or lawyer-vetted statement. He knew it and Sportsnet knew it. Tim said something along the lines of, "Well, if Dad's not going to read your statement and you are getting heat from the sponsors, then it's not that hard a decision." There was talk about Dad's legacy. People didn't understand that if Dad did what they asked, his legacy would be ruined. Or maybe they did.

Tim and I never entered the conversation or debate with Dad on what he should do. I figured it like this: not many people watching would be upset with what Dad had to say. However, because of how media and communication work today, most people who became upset learned about it from the aftermath of the media reportage. I get it. I knew Dad had said many things that had upset people, but this time it was different. Not so much with the people, but with the corporations. This was their chance to do what they had been trying to do for years: oust Dad. In the past they knew he had a tremendous following, plus he brought in big bucks in advertising time before Coach's Corner. How many commercials did you have to sit through before he finally came on? You always had time to refresh your beverage. But now it was different. I believe it was their agenda to start eliminating a lot of the higher-paid talent, and if so, it would only be logical that Dad would be at the top of their hit list.

I got home from Ottawa that Sunday night and, fortunately or unfortunately, missed Ron on his Hometown Hockey pre-game show giving his original speech addressing what I've come to call "Poppygate." Let's face it, we were prepared to hear what Ron was going to say on HNiC, but what he said that Sunday would have opened my eyes to how viral this was all going to go.

Granted, it was probably scripted by the powers-that-be, but still, to hear such words coming from Ron as "his remarks were hurtful, discriminatory . . . flat-out wrong . . . it was a really good lesson for Don and me . . ." was a real shocker. I watched the TV news that night to see the spin they would put on it. I am not a masochist, but we Cherrys have tough skin and can take the slings and arrows. We have had a lot of practice because of people commenting on his history of controversial remarks. The people who were always upset with him, calling him names, weren't my type of people anyway. I am always glad when those types are upset. However, the left-wing media has the gullible public's ear. If you want to see him stoke the fire of these types, google his speech in 2010 at the late Rob Ford's Toronto mayoral inauguration. He ended it by saying, ". . . and put that in your pipe, you left-wing kooks." It was classic and, needless to say, ruffled a lot of feathers. However, I was taught that if you want to be that way, you had better be prepared to take the backlash. You can't have your cake and eat it too—one of the many lessons I have learned from him, and will probably have to apply to this book.

So, on Monday morning, November 11, 2019, Dad called me and said it was over. He was to be on all the news channels that day, but wanted to call me before it was announced. He confirmed he had met with the Rogers/Sportsnet brass that Sunday. He really had no animosity toward them. As he said, they too were only doing their job. They asked him to apologize, which he said he would not do. However, he said he would go back on air and try to explain what he meant better. They didn't want that, for they knew that was coming awfully close to what they were asking. And then there was officially no more Coach's Corner.

The narrative that Rogers/Sportsnet and Ron put out to the rest of the media was that all Don had to do to keep his job was apologize, and he wouldn't. That is what a lot of the corporate media shills and people on social media jumped on—why didn't Don just say he was sorry, and then he would have gotten his job back? To me, there is no doubt Rogers wanted Dad gone, so they backed him into a corner knowing he wouldn't kneel to their demands. I believe many people in the corporate media knew there was more to the story about Dad's firing, but didn't bother looking into it and just went with the corporate narrative: "Don wouldn't say sorry." In the end I think what endears Dad to so many people is that they are tired of seeing celebrities and politicians get in trouble for saying something they genuinely mean, and when the shit hits the fan they come out with an insincere apology to keep their job.

When big companies are dependent on corporate marketing dollars they listen to those corporations, who in turn listen to social media, and we all know how reliable that is. "Those people" who were upset were not even the target market of advertisers on Coach's Corner, yet they caved to the noisy minority. If you said anything in Dad's defence, you would be labelled racist, xenophobic, etc., so who would want to take on that headache?

So, one more Canadian tradition is gone. Many people told me how hockey changed for them that day. Hockey fans had their Saturdays in a routine that revolved around 7:50 p.m. I even had my own. It was always nice that, no matter where I was, I could tune in and see my dad on TV Saturday nights. Men have told me jokingly that their wives were happy that Coach's Corner wasn't on any more, as they could now go out for dinners and movies on Saturday nights. They knew that no matter what time they got home, they could always tune in and get an update on the games, but there was nothing like watching a live Coach's Corner.

On that point, how much can one game be analyzed? Every game is dissected to death by four or more people talking over one another now. It's painful. Dad always had fun stuff to show and inside pointers to discuss, things that, with all these experts, no one has picked up on. He always showed pictures of winners of minor hockey tournaments and paid homage to the great work the police, firefighters, and first responders do, let alone recognize the pictures of fallen soldiers. All that stopped because some people took offence to him questioning why more people don't wear poppies.

CHAPTER 2

REMEMBRANCE DAY, NOVEMBER 11, 2019

S o, it was the end of Coach's Corner. The official word was given on November 11, 2019: Remembrance Day. The media was parked outside of Dad's house, and many were invited in to sit down with him. The slant they would all take on the issue was predictable. Strangely enough, I received a message at the Don Cherry's Pet Rescue Foundation email address that Fox News wanted to get hold of Dad. *Yippee*, I said to myself. *If there is one media outlet that may give him a fair shake and not put a negative spin on it, it would be Tucker Carlson's.* Sure, I got a lot of requests that I ignored, but this one was special.

I called Dad and said that, if there was one interview he did, this should be it. I knew my brother Tim would not be pleased, for he could see the potential of it being a disaster. Like most news outlets, they can put a spin on just about anything to make their point. I knew Dad was a pro at handling himself with interviewers, but one slip-up would have added fuel to the fire. This would have given the left-wing media even more fodder to bury Dad with. One thing I know about Dad is that he recognizes when he's being baited and led down a garden path into answering questions in a truthful way, which could lead to even more controversy. He had been interviewed hundreds of times throughout the years, so he was a pro at dodging questions when he knew the interviewer had an ulterior motive and/or agenda. He once explained to me that most interviewers' strategy is pretending to be nice and friendly while nodding their heads in agreement, then, when they think they have lulled you into a false sense of security, they pounce with a question from left field, one that was the real reason and motive behind the interview in the first place. This catches you off guard and you're taken aback, which may lead you to stumble over answers and look foolish. This ambush journalism happens all the time.

Fox News is like no other media outlet in Canada. We knew they would emphasize the point that this issue had the Canadian media in an uproar. However, with my encouragement, Dad agreed to go on Fox, his favourite news channel.

It surprised me how much Tucker knew of the situation, and he kept repeating that he didn't see what the big deal was. He kept trying to figure out the dynamics and logic of firing a paid TV commentator expressing his opinion of wanting more people to wear a symbol that shows their support of soldiers who died in Canadian wars (they don't do the poppy thing in the States). It was hard for him to fathom. (Welcome to my world, Tucker.) Dad got through it with flying colours, despite the ample opportunity Tucker gave him to throw a lot of people under the bus. He used restraint and resisted the temptation, which I was proud of him for doing. I don't think I could have.[2]

It should be noted that to some degree Tim was correct in his apprehension about Dad going on Fox News. Three years later, he still gets messages on his social media outlet bashing him for going on with Tucker Carlson. For instance, in September of 2022, a woman wrote on his *Rock'em Sock'em* Hockey Facebook page that she used to love Dad, but since he went on Tucker's show she figured Tucker was now interfering in Canadian politics. (I don't understand how she'd come to that conclusion and now thinks Dad is a "scumbag.") I try not to go on Dad's Facebook page because of posts like this; however, when I do I usually regret it.

Take the time I went on because I wanted a picture of Dad wearing a crown that the people at the Stratford Festival gave him when he did his King Lear imitation for HNiC. Rather than bother Tim, who had posted this picture, I thought I'd take it off the *Rock'em Sock'em* site—big mistake. When I go on social media, I can't seem to resist reading the comments. It's

---

[2]   Brehm, Mike. "Don Cherry Tells Tucker Carlson on Fox News He Was Fired for Using the Words, 'You People.'" USA TODAY, 13 Nov. 2019, https://www.usatoday.com/story/sports/nhl/2019/11/12/don-cherry-tucker-carlson-fox-news-show-hockey-night-canada/2582747001/

like trying not to look at a traffic accident as you drive by—you know you shouldn't but you can't help yourself. There, under the shot of Dad wearing the crown, a woman had commented, "Aren't you dead yet?" When Tim and I read such nonsense our immediate reaction is to write something back, but it's best left alone. Nothing hurts more than being ignored, but it's tough to do. So I thought I'd bring in my own keyboard warrior friends from Don Cherry's Pet Rescue Foundation. I mentioned to them how some people can be so hurtful. I knew that no one knows how to manipulate social media better than the pet-rescue world. They came through for me in spades, and I bet that commenter didn't even know where it came from.

That Remembrance Day, I got many calls from friends showing their support and expressing their disbelief that it was all to end like this. The most memorable was a call from Eugene Melnyk, at the time the owner of the Ottawa Senators. He was a guy who knew what it is like to take lots of slings and arrows from the press and public. He was once accused of paying in a roundabout way for an organ transplant he needed. This was not true at all, for I (once an employee of the Kidney Foundation of Canada and an organ donor myself) know how the system works. But since he was rich and in desperate need of the operation, which was successful, that was the rumour going around.

He always liked Dad for feeling his pain in owning the team in Ottawa and keeping it there. Despite Melnyk losing tons of money he kept the team in Ottawa, and yet he received little community appreciation for it. I could never figure this out, nor could Dad, and he said so many times on Coach's Corner. He always said that if he were Melnyk, he'd cut bait and move the team to Quebec.

When Melnyk called me initially, he asked for Dad's phone number to show his support. However, once he and I started talking we had a nice chat about the media and what it is like to deal with them. He was a smart guy (he passed away in 2022). He knew his audience and could tell I felt his pain, and he felt comfortable enough to vent to me. It was a spicy conversation, and he knew his rant would stay with me. I remember him liking my comment about Dad's philosophy regarding the press: "They're either at your feet or your throat." He was thrilled to hear that Dad was going on Fox News that night, and told me he'd be watching. Sure enough, I got a text with two thumbs up after the broadcast.

That day I taped all of Dad's TV interviews that were done in his house. They had the same theme and motive, which was to see who was going to be the first reporter to get Don Cherry to say the word that Canadians throughout the world are known for: "sorry." Sorry, not going to happen. It was amusing to see how many different ways they could ask the same question over and over. There was one interviewer who asked it three different ways, and the family had to finally step in and say, "He has answered your question three times now—enough."

What also motivated the closing of that interview was Dad sitting close to the lit fireplace (isn't that a metaphor for the predicament?). Normally that gas fireplace doesn't throw a lot of heat, but he was sitting close to it because it made a nice backdrop for the shot. There were so many interviews in the house that it was only fair to the reporters not to have the same background, so they had to move around his house. One setting was the solarium, and he has two fireplaces on the main floor, so they'd change the angles and the backdrops for different interviewers.

When he asked me how he thought it went the next day, I mentioned that his house looked great, very cozy and classy, and they showed off his collection of Royal Doulton's Toby mugs well.

It was also interesting how the news anchors led into the story. You'd think they'd have a little mercy, seeing that Dad was kind to them in opening up his home. He knew they had a job to do, and to me this was a kind gesture. His wife, Luba, offered them coffee, and when they were waiting for an interview outside she invited them in to warm up. Perhaps they had mistaken this kindness for weakness. Or maybe they thought that the Cherry family was being human to them so they would be kind. Trust me, we knew better than that. They would do their best to trip him up and try to get him to insinuate that his comments were directed at immigrants. He had his eyes wide open going into those interviews, knowing one slip-up would make even more headlines. He didn't falter or cave to any of them, no matter how hard they pushed. He kept saying the same thing over and over again.

It was entertaining listening to each interviewer's intro to the same story. They all tried to put a spin on it so it sounded like Dad was defending himself in their *exclusive* interview, which was far from the truth. All the interviews were endless; not one interviewer had an original question, and all were non-enlightening. Still, I must admit the intros were painful to hear (other than Tucker's). Words such as *disgraced, racist, xenophobic,* and, of course, the most used one, *divisive,* were all used as headliners going into the interviews. I guess that's what it takes to sucker the viewers in, which is the name of the game.

However, I'll give credit where credit is due. On CTV, reporter Andria Case did a short story on Dad starting up the Grapevine Podcast shortly after Coach's Corner was cancelled. In it, she never used the buzzwords *disgraced, racist,* or *xenophobic* to describe Dad. She just talked about the podcast. It was refreshing.

Again, the agenda for most people wanting him to respond to his dismissal was to get him to say he was sorry. Sorry for what? I guess the public could then fill in the blanks for their own amusement. It doesn't matter, for it wasn't going to happen. The focus of this book is on Don Cherry, including his life philosophies. Fortunately or unfortunately, they are also mine.

The whole exercise of saying you're sorry is overrated. We are a culture who apologizes and all is forgiven. This translates as, "You can do any bad thing you want and all you have to do is say you're sorry to make it right." Look what "granola parents" teach their children. How often have you heard parents say to their child, "Say you're sorry"? Their obedient kid then says sorry, but insincerely. To me (and maybe I am wrong—it wouldn't be the first time), this reinforces to the child that you can do anything wrong as long as you say sorry after. Clobber your friend over the head with a toy truck, and when he cries just say you're sorry and move on to the next time. A child has an impressionable brain at the early stages of life. When my son Del was young and said he was sorry to me about something, I'd tell him he was only sorry he got caught. If he'd argue with me about his sincerity, I'd ask him what he was sorry for, and how he was going to change that behaviour in the future. One day he came to me and said he was sorry he didn't cut the grass like I had asked him to. I told him, "Rather than being sorry about it, tell me why you didn't do it, and how you are going to ensure it won't happen again." I would then tell him the consequences of what would happen if the grass didn't get cut the next Saturday.

Parents are brainwashed into this "sorry" mentality. Personally, I feel they say it to sound like an accountable parent to other parents. We all ıw how parental peer pressure is. It's a strong force that is hard to resist (or not cave in to), but parents have to extrapolate their teachings to their children into adulthood. As Dr. Phil says, your job as a parent is preparing your child for the real world, not protecting them from it, as many parents do. They think solving their kids' problems is a sign of love, and therefore we have all these brats with no coping skills. These are the same parents who are always harping at their kids to say they are sorry. So what is the outcome if you are accused of political incorrectness, racism, or sexism— pick your poison—just say you're sorry and all is forgiven?

A perfect instance of this "sorry mentality," or recanting one's opinion to keep a job, was on CTV's show *The Social*, featuring Jess Allen commenting on Dad's dismissal. I loved the late Canadian author and journalist Rex Murphy's thoughts on her rant, saying it was like "chickadees sneering at an eagle."[3] Does it get any better than that? In her tirade, Ms. Allen claimed she doesn't "worship at the altar of hockey," and that she found, in her experience, that those who did "all tend to be white boys who weren't, let's say, very nice." She also added, "They were not generally thoughtful. They were often bullies. Their parents were able to afford to spend five thousand dollars a year on minor hockey. Five thousand dollars is a lot of money. You can do other things besides spending time in an arena. They could go on a trip and learn about the world, see other things, eh? The world is a big place. Get outside the bubble."

She then brought it full circle to Dad, saying, "For me, Don Cherry is the walking and talking representative of that type." She continued by acknowledging that, though he has done some good things, he is "still a bigot and a misogynist." I guess she knew better than to call him a racist, as many at that time were doing, for it was she who chose to single out a race with her "white boys" comment. To allow her to keep her job, CTV made her apologize by saying, "I do have regrets. I regret saying that my experiences were personal instead of underlining that they were specific

---

3   Murphy, Rex: Shame on You Sportsnet. Don Cherry Deserved Much, Much Better." *Nationalpost*, 16 Nov. 2019, https://nationalpost.com/opinion/rex-murphy-shame-on-you-sportsnet-don-cherry-deserved-much-much-better

episodes from determined moments with particular individuals."[4] Read between the lines with that one.

I wonder what Ms. Allen's answer would be if you had a glass of wine with her (after she mopped the floor with herself to keep her job) and asked, "Are you really sorry?" The question the Cherry family was asked was: "Should Jesse Allen have gotten fired?" Of course not. If that's how she feels, why should she hide those feelings? Let the free market dictate her future. If people had gotten angry enough at her and stopped watching the show, CTV should have let her go, for she would have been affecting their bottom line. Though she is getting paid to give her opinions, it is evident that her employer makes her toe the line if she wants to keep her job. In contrast, what happened to HNiC's ratings after Dad left? According to the figures from Numeris, Canada's broadcast measurement firm, HNiC's ratings took an immediate hit in the wake of Dad's firing. In the two weeks following, the eastern broadcast of HNiC failed to make the top 30 TV shows ranked by Numeris.[5]

The story of Tara Slone, who used to co-host the pre-game show Hometown Hockey with Ron before it was cancelled, is also really sad. Here was a person who spewed her venom on social media three years after the fact. I guess she had to be relevant, and to trend on social media you just need to mention Don Cherry (so they tell me). It's too bad she didn't give us quotes about what he said to her to back up her claims that "he is a bigot and has no place on national television with a national platform."[6] She even insinuated that Dad was jealous of Ron. She has no worries from the Cherry family about being misquoted or getting sued—we don't care. What I will say about her is this: I believe nothing is more demeaning than being hired as a token. One would have to wonder how being an actress, morning TV host, singer in a rock band, or a reality TV contestant would

---

[4]   The Canadian Press: CTV, Jessica Allen Apologize for Hockey Remarks After Don Cherry's Firing." *CBC*, 15 Nov. 2019, https://www.cbc.ca/news/entertainment/allen-cherry-hockey-apology-1.5361608

[5]   Lilley, Brian: Dumping Don Cherry Hurting HNIC Ratings." *Torontosun*, 25 Dec. 2019, https://torontosun.com/opinion/columnists/lilley-dumping-don-cherry-hurting-hnic-ratings

[6]   Daniell, Mark: "Former Sportsnet Host Tara Slone Blasts 'bigot' Don Cherry." *Torontosun*, 21 Oct. 2022, https://torontosun.com/entertainment/television/former-sportsnet-host-tara-slone-blasts-bigot-don-cherry

qualify you for being a sportscaster, or whatever you want to call it that she did with Ron. One would wonder where she got all her hockey knowledge from. She even said that "hosting Hometown Hockey was the longest I have ever held one job." Which is something I wouldn't brag about.

After watching all of Dad's interviews that Monday I was mentally and physically exhausted. I can only imagine how he felt. I called him up the next morning and told him how proud I was of him. He kept his cool and treated each interrogator like it was the first time he had heard their stupid questions. He treated them all with respect, with not one iota of contempt in his voice. That must have taken great restraint.

CHAPTER 3

POPPYGATE FALLOUT

I was always taught never to bite the hand that feeds you, and Rogers/Sportsnet/CBC paid Dad well. However, sometimes when that dog bites it is hard to control. Dad told me at one point that they had advised him that they would prefer him to stop showing images of soldiers who had been killed. They probably thought that if they forced this issue, all Dad had to do was let it be known to the press that he was being forced to discontinue this tradition, which would not go over well. It was a no-win situation for them, so you can't blame them for being resentful.

Though they viewed him as an irritant, they realized he was a cash cow. Those commercials leading up to Coach's Corner were costly. They knew his presence at special events, such as outdoor games and exhibitions like Kraft Hockeyville, gave them legitimacy. People would watch if he and Ron showed up, which meant revenue to them. His syndicated radio show, a Roger's production, was on over 100 stations across Canada. It was one of the country's longest-running radio shows, and it ended in 2019 after 35 years. Dad and his co-host Brian Williams agreed to end the show while it was on top. Thank goodness they made that call at the beginning of the 2019–20 hockey season or it too would have been another casualty of Poppygate. In saying all this, we the Cherry family have to look back in appreciation of CBC and Rogers, who allowed Dad be Don Cherry and get paid handsomely for it. Without them, he would not have become one of the most recognizable forces in Canada.

The Canadian Hockey League

Everyone who knows hockey knows how Dad promoted the CHL. There are many aspects of how he relates to this significant developer of NHL players. One was the concept started in 1996 of having a CHL/NHL Top Prospect game played annually. They approached Dad and Bobby Orr with the idea of coaching against each other, and they agreed. They had a tradition: both put up $100 to see who would win, Team Orr or Team Cherry. Please note they never received a dime for their time; though, once again, it later became a huge cash generator for all parties involved but them.

I remember attending the first game in the old Maple Leaf Gardens in Toronto. Hardly anyone showed up. No one got the concept that all the top prospects of the CHL would get to show off their talents to the world and, more importantly, NHL scouts. For years fans were so scarce that our family would sit behind the bench to make the Gardens look like spectators were showing up. I brought my three-year-old son Del to a game, and we took the seats beside the bench along the glass so he could play with his Buzz Lightyear figurines along the top of the boards. But in the last years that we went, we were lucky to get a seat. My, how things change.

Fast-forward to December 2019. The game is being played in Hamilton and Dad and Bobby are scheduled to coach. After Poppygate, Dad started calling the CHL offices to see about his participation in the game. No reply. We could see the writing on the wall, and Dad decided to let them off the hook by having a conversation with them about the possibility of their sponsors or fans questioning them about having him back. He didn't want to distract from the event, so he said he couldn't make it. With no Cherry, you know Bobby wasn't going to show up.

Not even Brian Kilrea, Dad's long-time friend, teammate, and assistant coach, was willing to show up. I wondered at what time the CHL made their decision that it was not in their best interest to host the return of the Cherry/Orr teams. It just so happens that I knew the owner of the company that made the sweaters for this event. I wanted to call him and ask what the new names of the teams were, and when he had gotten the order. However, I didn't want to put him on the spot so I didn't make the call. It's still hard to believe that after 23 years of starting the tradition of Orr vs. Cherry they could so easily change the names on the sweaters. Such is life.

Western Hockey League/Kidney Foundation of Canada

I used to work part-time for the western branches of the Kidney Foundation of Canada. I started a campaign called "WHL Suits Up With Don Cherry" to promote organ transplants in Canada and raise funds for the KFoC. The teams wore custom sweaters in the likeness of Dad's trademark suits during the games, which were later auctioned off. In three years it raised close to $600,000. Well, you guessed it, after Poppygate it was decided to remove his name from the campaign banner. Plus, I was not invited to any of the games, as I had been in previous years. I was even told that one, just one, volunteer said that if I went to the game she would no longer volunteer, and they caved. This is another example of sponsors, teams, and leagues not wanting to get into the fray for fear of some people and the media accusing them of supporting racism. I knew it was with a heavy heart that they contacted me in January 2020 and told me I'd have to miss the campaign kickoff in Edmonton. I have no ill will, and I can't blame them. But it goes to prove there was much more to the fallout from Poppygate than meets the eye. Take, for instance, how it affected Don Cherry's Pet Rescue Foundation.

Don Cherry's Pet Rescue Foundation

In 2014, I started a not-for-profit organization called Don Cherry's Pet Rescue Foundation after a business associate approached me about creating a line of dog treats. He had been successful in manufacturing children's products, and I had mentioned that when he wanted to tackle the pet industry he should give me a call. I've been involved in the pet industry throughout my life. I am a dog groomer by trade and I still do it to this day. I went to college in Kingston, Ontario, to become an animal-care technician; I worked in many pet stores, at a racetrack, and at a zoo; and had my own line of pet specialty-care cassettes.

The call came in 2014 inquiring about having Don Cherry as a spokesperson for this line of pet treats. Dad had no interest, and they couldn't afford his endorsement fees anyway. I was asked what it would take to get him on board. I suggested starting up a foundation so the money he would normally get as endorsement fees would be given away as grants. It was a good fit, with him always talking about his bull terrier

Blue and supporting many fundraisers for animal causes. I knew he wanted to do more for people on the front lines of saving animals, so this was an avenue he could take to make his vision a reality. I knew I would be the only one who could propose such an idea. When pitching to a person like Dad, it's all in the delivery and spin you put on it. I knew if I focused more on the foundation and its good work, as opposed to the treats themselves, he'd agree to it.

Though these marketing "gurus" thought they had it all figured out, the last thing the pet industry needed was another dog treat. I knew we were in trouble when the first flavours they came up with were "cinnamon bun" and "white fish"—go figure. With flavours like these, I knew the packaging needed more than the Don Cherry's Pet Rescue Foundation logo on it. I knew we needed to develop something that no one else was doing. I came up with the idea of using pictures of rescue dogs on the packaging. Each one had an unbelievable survivor story, which we detailed on our foundation's website. Though the concept was great, who would have anticipated the resistance we received? For instance, Dad had fallen in love with a picture of a rescued one-eyed Cane Corso pup that I knew of. He wanted this to be the first dog on the packaging. The problem was, when we went to put the packaging in Walmart, their powers-that-be said it was offensive to see such a dog on the packaging, and they didn't want it in their store. We told them that Don wanted it and, seeing they had scheduled a grand kick-off event with Dad attending, they gave in. The public thought it was a great concept, and so did I.

This wouldn't be the last time Walmart had issues with the foundation. Fast-forward to 2019, after the Poppygate saga. They informed the suppliers of these treats that they did not want the foundation's logo in their store. This is the same store that, at the time, sold 14 items heralding Michael Vick's accomplishments in the NFL. He was an ex-convict, having been convicted on U.S. federal and state charges related to illegal dog fighting via his Bad Newz Kennels. This kennel raised, housed, and trained over 70 pitbulls; staged dog fights; killed underperforming dogs by drowning, electrocution, and hanging; and ran a high-stakes gambling ring with purses up to $26,000. Walmart had no problem selling this guy's stuff, but took issue with selling items with Don Cherry's Pet Rescue Foundation's logo. Do you see how corporations are contradictory in terms and logic?

Though having this logo on the packaging was an asset in marketing strategy, there were some stores where this was an issue; another one was Dollarama. Their issue came long before Poppygate, and I didn't see it coming. I had final approval on all the packaging. It was explained to me in an email that Dollarama wanted to use a logo that didn't include Dad's picture. I didn't think much of it at the time, for I was out west travelling for the Kidney Foundation of Canada, promoting organ transplants. I was tired on the road, and not as sharp as I should have been. It wasn't until I got back home and was rested that it dawned on me that their head office was in Quebec. I extrapolated and concluded that it was probably a Don vs. the French issue. Go figure that! Dad often said that sometimes there are advantages with being associated with him, and sometimes not so much. We sure learned that fast, for in 2020 Don Cherry's Pet Rescue Foundation stopped receiving funds from this dog treat supply company—another casualty of Poppygate.

CHAPTER 4

RON

*T*he stories about Dad and Ron are endless. People would always ask me about their relationship, before and after Poppygate. Most wanted to know if they were really friends, because on TV you'd swear there was no love lost between them at times. I'd always answer them truthfully. It was a unique relationship and a hard one to describe, and I envied it to some degree. Let's face it, it's easy to figure out that Ron is very liberal in his thinking—or, as it's been described to me, he's a "limousine liberal," which I thought was clever. Two of Dad's closest relationships, in Mike Milbury and Ron, were in many ways ideologically opposite, yet they were always good friends. Does this not say something about my father? Sure, he can be judgemental, but common sense prevails when it comes to friendships. Dad doesn't have many friends. He may know lots of people, but few and far between are the ones allowed in his inner circle. His little black book (yes, he actually has one, as he doesn't do computers or cell phones) and the contacts in it are priceless, but most are acquaintances.

He and Ron never socialized outside of hockey duties, but think of the time they spent together during them. Remember, for the semi-finals and finals they were usually at those games, not back in the CBC studios. That is a lot of travelling together, and nothing tests a relationship more than that. One stipulation they had for any hotel they stayed in was that it had to have a sauna. Dad is big on saunas. One time they were staying with the whole HNiC crew at a particular hotel, and they found out it had no sauna. They checked out and went to another one. Dad told me one time he opened the door of a hotel sauna and a person fell out. Apparently the door had become stuck from the inside, and he would have been a goner if Dad hadn't come in.

Dad prided himself on how long he could stay in one. During one session, a man came in at the same time as Dad who must have had that same value system. Dad told me it turned into a battle of wills about who was going to leave first. He never told me the outcome, but knowing Dad he would have been pretty dehydrated at the end of that steam. He was never one to drink water, but I'm sure the beer tasted pretty good afterwards. As he terms it when he has a thirst on, it wouldn't have touched his throat going down.

Mom and Dad had their own rituals about drinking beer, and I have adopted both their philosophies. Mom always drank beer in a wine glass, which only makes sense. It's thinner glass, which means it keeps the beer colder than a thick glass or mug, plus your fingers never touch where the beer is to warm it up, and it's lighter. And it's nice to see where the cold beer makes a frosty film on the glass, chilling it.

Speaking of chilled glasses, here's a habit he taught Ron. When drinking draft while sitting at a bar, usually the bartender asks if you want another after your last swig, at which point they take your empty mug and refill it. Dad would order before his last swig, so the bartender would grab a new chilled glass and fills it. Dad would then take his last gulp and hand over the old glass in exchange for his new frosty mug. One night Ron kept drinking out of the same warm, fingerprinted glass until Dad said, "Do you not see what's going on here?" There is a science and rules to everything for Dad, especially when it comes to eating and drinking. He will always pour his own beer from a bottle, for he hates a tall head on it. I know a lot of beer connoisseurs say it releases the gasses, but Dad's theory is, "If I wanted a milkshake, I'd order one."

If you choose to drink socially with Dad, know that he has many rules. For instance, you cannot go out with him if you've had dinner beforehand. There have been times on the road that Ron would go out for dinner with other people, then call Dad to tell him he's back. If Dad suspected he'd had dinner with them, he'd feel the night was ruined, stay in his room, and have a few by himself. If you go out with him for a few beers in the evening, you can't sit with him if you order food, even appetizers. One time an executive producer of HNiC saw Dad at a bar and came over to his table, bringing his chicken wings with him, and Dad asked him to leave. Peanuts, chips, and popcorn are OK, but if you have anything else, even cheese and crackers, it's a sign that the night is over.

When you do go out for dinner with Dad, he is one of those people who thinks everyone has ordered something better than him. He'll look at everyone's entrée and say, "I should've ordered that. What is it? That's what I am ordering next time." If he's directing this at me, it's then that I usually split my food with him.

He is the perfect person to wait on in a restaurant. No matter how bad the food is, he will never complain. If I say one thing about my drink or food, he'll shush me in case the waitstaff hear and get their feelings hurt. I once asked a waiter if they served my favourite drink, an Arnold Palmer, and when they said no Dad told me I'd made the server feel bad.

One time he was having dinner with Scotty Bowman, among a bunch of people. They all had soup as an appetizer, and Scotty complained to the waiter that it tasted burnt. The waiter asked if anyone else's soup was burnt, and they all said it was fine; plus, you'd figure it came from the same pot. At the end of the meal Scotty got a free dessert while everyone else got nothing. It bothered Dad that a complainer got rewarded and went dessertless. If you even ask the waiter questions about the food, he will show his irritation. The ones that really send him through the roof are "Is it fresh?" and "What do you recommend?" Because I worked in the restaurant industry, I like to engage the wait staff as little as possible. Trust me, they are only humouring you, pretending they are hanging on to your every word or, worse yet, banter. Remember, awful things can happen to your food before you get it. Believe me, I've been there. We franchised our restaurants, Don Cherry's Sports Grills, across Canada, which I assisted in, so I know the industry pretty well.

When on the road with Ron, Dad would usually bring sandwiches in his suitcase for late-night snacks. After one game he realized he didn't have any, so they stopped at a sandwich shop. Ron asked for tuna, and since it was late at night and the server didn't want to keep it for the next day, he emptied the whole container onto the bun. Dad saw there was no more tuna and ordered chicken salad, which came with the basic amount on it. Much to Dad's chagrin, Ron's was triple his sandwich in thickness which, as you can imagine, made Ron's night. He rubbed it in mercilessly, saying how much he was looking forward to digging into his oh-so thick sandwich when they got back to the hotel.

Most nights they'd go to Ron's room to watch TV and eat, but it was late so they called it. When Dad opened his bag back in his room, there was Ron's triple-thick sandwich. To this day Dad denies he switched the bags, but Ron and I both know that is something he'd do.

Dad told me that, years later, Ron told him that he really believed Dad would bring his tuna sandwich to him that night. That surprised me, knowing Dad as well as he does. I believe that, if the roles were reversed, Ron would have brought Dad his thicker sandwich. I also believe there was no question that Dad would never have given back that sandwich. Knowing what kind of guy Ron truly is made it that much harder to watch him talk about Dad and the poppy debacle on TV.

In this next observation about Dad, I can see how I am my father's daughter. There was never a question that when Dad and Ron met to watch TV on the road, it was going to be in Ron's room. Dad told me that Ron's room was always neat. The bathroom counter held his toothpaste and toothbrush and that's it. I've seen Dad's hotel counter, and there's never one empty square inch. He is definitely high maintenance and does not travel lightly. Unfortunately, I have inherited that gene. I not only use up the whole counter, but I also need to put stuff in the toilet tank, that's how much junk I have. I used to do a lot of business travel with a work colleague. She and I would go to the same work functions, and she would bring everything she needed in a carry-on. I would always tick her off by checking my luggage. My toiletries, makeup, and hair products alone could fill one side of a suitcase. As with Dad and Ron, if we were to meet in a room, it would be her's. I would even use up the second bed in my room for all my stuff.

Before every playoff run, Dad would be determined to eliminate half of the items in his suitcase. Once I asked Mom where Dad was, and she said, "He's trying to do his playoff purge, and you know he can't do it." Sure enough, he came downstairs and claimed he just didn't understand how everyone travels so light. I truly felt his pain. We both tell hotel clerks at check-in that we do not want service in our rooms during our stay—we're embarrassed about how junkie our rooms are. Yet when we leave, the rooms are spotless and our newspapers and magazines are neatly stacked in the tub with all the towels, along with a big tip.

I have been in many airports with Dad, and it is not fun. I still get chills when I think of one trip in the early nineties, when phones and cameras were combining. We were running late for our plane and an older couple asked if I'd take a picture with them and Dad. I kept pressing the button and it wouldn't click. I started mumbling to myself about how we need this like a hole in the head, and other nasty things. I politely said to them, "It's not working, I think something is wrong." The guy looks at it and says, "Oh, you have it on video." I turned white as a ghost. Dad asked me if I was all right. I felt lightheaded, and just shook my head. Thank goodness there was no social media yet to post my nastiness. I learned my lesson early about phones being recorders.

When Ron and Dad were travelling together, people would often mistake them for undercover policemen. It makes sense: they look like old cop, new cop, travelling in shirts and ties. Many times people came up to them asking for assistance, which they always obliged, or got them the help they needed.

Remember, they have been together since long before cameras were on phones. They evolved with it, as they were constantly being asked to have their picture taken with fans. One time they were taking a picture with a lady, and Ron offered the recommendation to turn the camera sideways for a wider shot. The woman said, "Yes, I know I put on some weight." The more he said that wasn't what he meant, the more embarrassed she felt. These incidents were why Dad called Ron "old silver tongue."

Jim Cuddy of Blue Rodeo once travelled with them, for he's a friend of Ron's. He sat beside us at a Leafs game, and the friend I was with kept trying to make small talk with him, and he was not receptive. During intermission I said to my buddy, "Can't you take a hint? He doesn't want to talk to you." We switched seats and I sat beside Jim in silence. Apparently he was relegated to cameraman when he was in airports with Dad and Ron, which he didn't appreciate. He eventually refused to play photographer. It was always nice to see people brought back to reality when they were around those two.

They say nothing causes more discontent among family members and friends than season tickets and cottages. Dad owned six season tickets, which he shared. When I got a pair, I liked to sit in the aisle seat. Del was always on edge if we'd be sitting in the wrong seats—some hoity-toity person would invariably along and tell me gruffly, "You're in my seat." I'd look up and say, "Are they *your* seats, or someone else's?" One guy informed me with attitude that they were Ron MacLean's, so I told him as I was moving over to tell Ron that Cindy says hello. It's no wonder my son didn't like going to the games with me. One time I was sitting beside some idiots who were incessantly yelling and screaming. I asked them if they were enjoying the game, and how they got their tickets. From scalpers, they said. Yikes. Needless to say, I found out who sold our tickets to scalpers to resell, and they heard about it.

I once went to a Leafs game with my husband and son, Tim and his wife, and my cousin, who was the assistant coach of the Mississauga IceDogs, a Major Junior A team in the Ontario Hockey League (OHL). A drunk behind us dribbled his rye and ginger all down our backs as he was getting through his row to his seat. I thought better of saying anything to avoid trouble, but my cousin, now with a wet shirt, asked him to say sorry. He replied no, and my cousin asked him nicely to say he was sorry three times, and he still refused. My cousin grabbed him by his shirt and flipped him over. With the guy's head on the pavement and feet in the air, he was still being told to say he was sorry. I told my cousin that I didn't think he could talk and to let him go, so he lifted him up and plopped him down into his seat. We were all in shock, including the drunk, but no one said a word. Security was heading over, so I told my cousin that he'd better take off, which he did. Security arrived and demanded the drunk and one of us to go down to their office, and I volunteered.

Once there they asked what the problem was, and I said, "He spilled drinks on us and wouldn't say he was sorry." A guard asked the drunk if that was what happened, and he said yes. That was when I noticed he was bleeding from where his wire-rim glasses had cut into his temple. It was explained to me that someone can't get beat up because they have bad manners, and I said, "I know, but that's what happened." They asked him if he wanted to lay charges, and he said he just wanted to watch the rest of the game. We both did the walk of shame back to our seats and not another word was spoken about it.

When I got home from the game I saw the blinking light on my answering machine. It was a message from a friend we shared the tickets with, who was sitting somewhere else for the game that night, asking what all the commotion was about. I called him back even though it was late and said it wasn't that big of a deal, asked how he had seen it, and he informed me that they had put it up on the jumbotron. I was more upset about that than the scuffle. I heard his wife laughing in the background and knew he was only trying to upset me. Funny guy.

Dad and Ron's scenarios on planes are always amusing. You know how some people put their seat back the whole way and now you're cramped? If it was done to Ron, Dad would take his newspaper and hit the offender, who would usually they think it was Ron who did it. If they looked back at Dad, he would point at Ron. When Dad was cramped because the idiot in front of him put his seat back, Dad would always wait until they were asleep then *whack*, slam his the tray up hard. He'd do it three or four times while they were trying to sleep. I have adopted this strategy too, and feel good when I do it.

Speaking about sleeping on the plane, Ron is one of the lucky people who can do this. I have inherited the gene from Dad that won't let us. There is something vulnerable about a person sleeping and I would never let myself be put in that position. Plus, I could not risk the chance of drooling. Dad has told me stories of Ron sleeping with a bit of drool on his face: when people walked by, Dad pointed out, "Yeah, that's Ron MacLean, big TV star. What do you think of him now? Not's so hot, eh?" Everyone would giggle and walk away.

One time Ron fell asleep before the plane even took off. They were on the tarmac for over an hour as he slept. People like Dad and me envy people who can sleep on a plane, so if Dad has the opportunity to even things up, he takes it. The plane still hadn't taken off, but Dad nudged Ron awake and told him they'd arrived. Poor Ron started getting up to go with everyone, including Dad, having a good laugh at Ron's expense.

On another occasion, Ron accidentally called a flight attendant "dear." Dad, in a rather loud voice, asked Ron, "Did you call this young lady *dear?*" She piped up, "Yes, and I heard that!" Dad said, "He says it all the time." Ron is one of the most non-condescending guys you'll ever meet, yet Dad loved to set him up so.

Ron and Dad are both avid readers, but Dad had a problem with the magazines Ron would buy, those muscle and lifestyle ones. Dad would see half-naked men in them and want Ron to not hold them up so he wouldn't have to see the pictures. If Ron was reading and Dad asked him a question, Ron would put his finger on the spot he stopped reading and hold it there for the whole conversation. Finally, Dad asked him (in a mean way, I'm sure), "How stupid are you that you can't remember where you stopped reading on a page?" Dad said this didn't deter Ron, so he stopped talking to him, which might have been the plan all along. Ron knew it didn't take much for Dad to be irritated.

One time they were leaving a Toronto pay-parking lot late at night. The cost was $4.50, and Ron gave the attendant a five-dollar bill and told him to buy himself a coffee. The guy fired the change back at Ron, so Dad yelled, to make Ron feel even worse, "Yes, my good man, buy yourself a hat or something frilly." The irony in this tale is that Ron is the biggest tipper Dad had ever seen. To add insult to injury, a squeegee man came up and wiped down Ron's window. Dad said, "You have to give him something now," so Ron generously handed him a ten-dollar bill. What did the guy do? Leaned in and said, "Thanks, Don," and Dad gave him the thumbs-up.

Ron knew Dad pretty well, and tried to assist people that might be going in to poke the bear. Take, for instance, the time Barry Melrose—the L.A. Kings' coach at the time—wanted Dad to apologize for something he said about him on air. What you need to know about Dad is that if he's gotten personal in his comments, there is usually a reason for it.

In the 1993 Campbell Conference finals, Pat Burns became enraged at Melrose when he thought he had sent Marty McSorley out on the ice to elbow Doug Gilmour. He actually charged the L.A. bench in retaliation. When the camera was on Melrose, he made a gesture of blowing up his cheeks and putting his hands around his waist to give the impression of a fat man coming to get him. When Melrose was asked his opinion about this scenario, he replied, "I thought he was trying to get a hot dog." Was this a reference to weight, or showboating to get more mustard for the hotdog?

Either way, Pat was a friend of Dad's, so game on. He went on Coach's Corner and proceeded to make fun of Melrose's infamous mullet, questioning if he was still trying to rebel against his father, and he ended with, "Who does he think he is, Billy Ray Cyrus?" Little did Dad know that HNiC was doing a live clip about both how Wendel Clark's and Barry Melrose's parents were together watching the game, as they had both come from Kelvington, Saskatchewan. As you can imagine, this caused some embarrassment to the senior Mr. Melrose, and Barry was not very happy.

The next time the HNiC crew were in L.A., Dad and Ron showed up to the morning skate. Ron got the word from their public-relations guy that Barry wanted to speak to him in their dressing room. Dad said he remembered wondering where Ron was off to. Barry told Ron that he wanted Dad to apologize. Ron told him, "Don't say anything to Don or he'll be relentless in his barrage of him." Ron knew this so well that he even told him that he was not even going to mention to Dad that they'd met. In all fairness I can see Barry's point, but another point has to be made here. He can dish it out pretty good, and is known for his critiques of people. He once said to a reporter that he was misquoted in saying that he thought all women in Toronto were short, explaining that he had instead said they were all ugly. It wasn't until two years later that Ron told Dad of this incident.

They had a unique relationship that lasted for decades, so to see it end the way it did was heartbreaking for the family. Dad is a unique guy, and I don't expect many people to have the same principles and honour that he does. In years past he had put his job on the line for Ron, but does that mean we should expect the same? I'd like to think so, but we all know that didn't happen. Ron was at a crossroads in his life. Should he sacrifice his career to be loyal to a friend? Dad believes that if this had happened twenty years ago Ron would have chosen loyalty and friendship, but not now. Dad said he knew he had changed. I guess things happen to you as you rise to fame and get used to money (though you can't say that about Dad). The thought of a career-limiting move is scary. Sportsnet made him play his hand in front of the whole hockey world. If he hadn't made his choice, there's no doubt he would be gone like Dad. Let's face it, they were probably the two highest-paid guys on Sportsnet. Ron had a decision to make, and we all know what he chose. I watched Ron's scripted rebuttal over at Tim's place, and Dad watched it alone in his basement. I don't believe we even called Dad up afterwards, or even discussed exactly what he said. We got the gist.

Obviously, Ron was reading from a script. In fact, I heard they made him repeat it several times in the taping. It's been said that Ron threw Dad under the bus, and I believe Sportsnet threw Ron under that same bus: they knew the ire of hockey fans would be directed more at Ron than the network. The left-wing media crucified Dad, but the real hockey fans spewed their venom at Ron. Tim and I took no joy in this. We have always seen Ron as part of our inner circle, which, trust me, is pretty small. To see him take those slings and arrows made me cringe, yet I knew he deserved it. Did he not see this coming? In a podcast interview that was not scripted by his bosses, Ron said, "There's so many elements to this . . . I had to pick what I felt [was] right over friendship. That just doesn't appeal to the heart. People want loyalty. People want friends for life."

Reading into this statement, it would seem to me that his bosses were still keeping an eye on what he would say about Dad.

In analyzing it (maybe a better word would be *rationalizing* it), I think Ron did what he had to do to keep his job. He is a lot younger than Dad, and he has a long way to go in his career. There is no doubt that Dad thinks differently than Ron, and they handle things in different ways.

I once tested the waters of how Dad was going to handle future situations with Ron. I had committed about 200 Ron and Don bobbleheads to a charity that had to be signed by both of them. I truly didn't know how Dad was going to react. He sat down at the table with all the bobbleheads ready to be signed, thinking about what to write. He asked, "Is Ron signing them?"

I replied, "He said he would."

"Good." was his only reply.

I then had to take them all over to Ron's place. I told Tim where I was going and got to thinking that maybe Ron would rather talk to my brother than me about the whole thing. So Tim took them over. When I asked him how it went, he didn't volunteer much info, and just said they'd had a good talk.

It's been years now since the blowup. Dad brings Ron up now and then, about how he handled the situation. He once asked me how I felt about it. He knows I am one tough cookie, vindictive and someone who holds a grudge, so I don't think he got the response he was expecting from me. I said, "I think Ron was as much a victim as you were." When he pressed me about it, I asked him, "What do you think Mom would say?" Sure, she would have been upset with him, but in the end her final comment would have been *Get over it*. He knows it, Tim knows it, and so do I—she always thought the world of Ron.

CHAPTER 5

XENOPHOBIC?

I YouTubed Dad's speech about poppies to see how long it went on for: one minute and thirty-six seconds. It had over 300,000 views and, since I'm a glutton for punishment, I thought I'd read some of the comments. Surprisingly, I got tired of scrolling down to find a negative comment, so I stopped. Where was all the negativity? I think people read into it what they wanted to, and as they knew Dad's past on certain topics or issues, they extrapolated what they wanted to believe.

The dictionary definition of "xenophobia" is "fear and/or hatred of strangers or foreigners." Without a doubt, this word is used most when the press are commenting on Dad's observations and/or comments. I feel no need to stick up for him in any way, for if you stick up for someone it usually means that the accused is confirmed in some way to be what you have labelled them. To say he has a fear or hatred of something or someone is laughable. It made for good press, and in the old days you'd say, "It sold a lot of newspapers." To take the slings and arrows from the media as he has and not care or worry about losing your job is what appeals to many people. They only wish they could speak their minds and not have to fear losing their income. For that fact alone, no matter what he said, even if people disagreed, they admired him for not worrying about it. He made it known that he saw himself as an older Anglo-Saxon white guy (a.k.a. a WASP) who anyone could say anything about and not worry about repercussions. His comments, on the other hand, were fodder for the press and his critics.

I know it's a cliché to say "don't take it personally." But people examine much of what Dad says to see how it could relate to them and take it personally. Could it be that they have a complex, or does the press want to make something out of it? For instance, he criticized Alex Ovechkin's "hot stick" goal celebration. Ovechkin had just scored his fiftieth goal of the season on Tampa Bay's rookie goalie Mike McKenna, making him the first player in Capitals' history to record three 50-goal seasons. He dropped his stick as if it were on fire and warmed his cold Russian hands with the imaginary burning kindling. His teammates, such as Mike Green and Nicklas Bäckström, did not join in on the showboating despite Alex inviting them over. Green said afterwards, "He told me he was going to do it. He wanted me to join in, but there was no way I'd join in on that. I just kind of stood back and let him do what he does."

Even his own coach, Bruce Boudreau, said he planned to speak to him about his orchestrated showmanship.

Ovechkin knew Dad would have something to say about this. After being pied in the face by his teammates in the dressing room, he had this to say: "[Don Cherry] is going to be pissed off, for sure . . . Can't wait till he says something about me. Saturday night. Coach's Rumour? Coach's Corner. It's pretty good."

It was Dad's inconsistency in picking what he would discuss on Coach's Corner that the public and players came to expect. Never one to shy away from a controversy, Dad had this to say: "Ovechkin . . . Alex. Is that his name? You're listening now. How would you like to be playing for Tampa? They're going through a nightmare season. It's in their building. They're being beaten 5–1 and you score on a rookie goalie. How do you think McKenna feels about this? Good guys like St. Louis said, 'He didn't have to embarrass us.' Good guys like Malone said, 'He's going to get a payback.' And Tocchet said the same thing, 'We didn't need something like that. You don't do that.' And you know? Everybody said he was taunting them. The guy's not a mean guy. He's not taunting them. He didn't mean to taunt them. But think how bad the rookie feels. You can't do stuff like that and not make people feel bad. But he's not a mean guy. He's just having a good time."

To a certain extent, he was trying to further Ovechkin's career by explaining to listeners that he was now a target, and the hockey gods have a way of giving payback. "Guys right now got you on a list. You're going to be very, very sorry, because somebody's going to cut you in half. And I hope it doesn't happen . . . He's going to get it, and when he gets it, it's going to be a goodie." In Dad's tradition of always adding words of wisdom to the kids, he added, "You don't act like this. This is goofy stuff . . . Don't you Canadian kids act like it."

Perhaps that reference to Canadian kids made the press interpret his whole tirade on Ovechkin as being anti-Russian. So no matter how Dad explained why what he did wasn't right, it became about him not liking Russians.

Dad might have also ruffled a lot of feathers by equating this showboating with the way soccer players carry on. Let's face it, he is not a soccer fan. He doesn't like how they excessively celebrate after they score, or the way they fake injuries on the field to get a penalty. When diving became the norm in hockey, he once again compared players rolling around on the ice and faking an injury to the same behaviour in soccer. Because soccer is such a popular sport in Europe, it was of course perceived as Dad knocking Europeans. I believe in the adage "if the shoe fits, wear it." If you don't think there is a correlation, then why get upset?

The truth is, he doesn't like any goofy celebration stunts, no matter who does it. Tie Domi rode his stick after a goal when he was with the Rangers and started to do a boxing-belt routine after his fights. Dad not only mentioned this on Coach's Corner, but since they were good friends, he personally addressed it. I find that the tough guys don't usually act like this, so perhaps Tie was channelling his inner Tiger Williams.

Dad calling out silly celebrations went to a whole new level when he called the Carolina Hurricanes a "bunch of jerks" in 2019. Their Storm Surge celebrations included a limbo stick line; duck, duck, goose; bowling; human dominoes; and their baseball surge. The upper management said it was to entertain the fans. I guess their hockey talents didn't cut it. As Americans often do with criticism, rather than whine about it, they embraced it and made it a whole marketing campaign. They were selling t-shirts, hats, and towels emblazoned with the "bunch of jerks" motto. When Dad was asked to apologize (sound familiar?), he came on even stronger, saying their fans were nothing but a bunch of front runners, starting to come out to the games not because of the team's antics to entertain their fans (acting like jerks), but because they started to win. He never got a free t-shirt.

He also called Evgeny Kuznetsov a jerk when he did his bird-flapping celebration against the Tampa Bay Lightning in 2019, after scoring the game-tying goal with 53 seconds remaining in the game. The press interpreted this as Dad knocking another Russian. Trust me, if a Canadian had done this Dad would have crucified them even more. The Lightning went on to win in overtime, with Kuznetsov on the ice for the game-winning goal. This led Dad to explain to kids watching that karma will always come back to haunt you, explaining that the Birdman's imitation only inspired the other team, which they should never do. When Kuznetsov was asked what he thought of Dad's comments, his opening statement was, "He's nice guy, you know? Sometimes I did watch his videos [when I was young in Russia]. If Don Cherry talking about you, that mean he thinking about you. Even if it's bad stuff, it's still good. He's legit. People love him."

So remember: when the press is crucifying him, the players know that he knows what he's talking about, and I'll believe players over the press anytime.

I believe Dad's problem with athletes overly celebrating comes from his passion for the other guy. He puts himself in their shoes. How would you feel? He admires players like Bobby Orr. When he scored and his teammates came up to him to celebrate, he'd almost push them away. After a goal, he was forever skating away with his stick and his head down—no need to rub his God-given talent in anyone's face. I call that class. Perhaps he believes a player should react to his achievements with, "Yeah, I've done it now and I'll do it again."

When you read these stories, I hope you don't think I'm justifying comments that draw ire from Dad's detractors. I'm only telling you how and why things happen, and by all means draw your own conclusions. I am sure this book will not change anyone's opinion about my dad, but perhaps it will cast a different light on him and the logic behind his actions.

For instance, he took a stand on not wanting to have European players on his team, the Mississauga IceDogs. He took a big hit on that decision, which he knew he would. His critics loved to point out that the franchise had a dismal start, but take it from me: it wasn't because they didn't have foreign hockey players in their rosters. That could be another chapter. The point is that he was permitting two more Canadian kids to fulfill their dreams of making it to the NHL.

Dad felt for the hockey parents who put money into their kids' possible careers, and he believed in giving them a shot over some kid who slid their way onto the team because they came from overseas. Parents here put tons of money back into our economy. If anyone has gone to tournaments, they know how much it costs: food, lodging, entry fees, wear and tear on your car, never mind that you may have to take time off work. They pay for new equipment and fees to the league; they sometimes have to pay a gate fee to watch their own kids play hockey. All these expenses drive that wheel into producing hockey players. And if your kid doesn't make it, well, you had a good time and that's it. I think, and so does Dad, that to have a kid imported to Canada to take the place of a Canadian kid is just not right. What has that player's family or European league done for Canada? They have given nothing back to this country that they want to play in to develop their skills further. They come here with just the shirts on their backs and the team does the rest. A lot of the time the team even has to pay for their trips back to Europe over the holidays. Does any of this type of compensation go to Canadian hockey parents? I think not.

Think about training camp. If the team has paid for the flight over for a Euro player they drafted and he is on the bubble with a Canadian kid, who do you think they will cut? The Canadian kid, of course. It's just plain economics. The team has invested money in the Euro, so do they want to admit they made a mistake? If you think hockey is just a sport, think again. It's a business. Try to explain this logic to a reporter who has an agenda of showing how Dad is xenophobic—not going to happen. It often fell on deaf ears, but the hockey world knew exactly what he meant and wouldn't touch that debate with a ten-foot pole. There are some topics that are not worth the hassle and the risk of being crucified for.

People thought he had something against Indigenous people, which was entirely false. Few people knew he put his job on the line when he coached in Colorado to keep Ron DeLorme on the team. Here was a player who was a Canadian Métis, instrumental in breaking barriers for Indigenous peoples in professional sports.

There was no love lost between Dad and their GM, Ray Miron, and the owners. After he was fired, he started to write a sports column. In one article he explained why he thought Ted Nolan and Mike Keenan might have trouble getting back into NHL coaching. There was a theory of racism on Nolan's part because he was Ojibwe. Clearly, Dad did not think this was the cause.

"The difference between me, Ted, and Mike is that I was ready to get out of coaching, and when I was let go I went down with guns blazing. [Hmmm, that sounds familiar.] I was not going quietly into the night when I got ripped by the owner's stepson [team president Armand Pohan] in a six-page press release. I went on TV with Dave Hodge on Hockey Night in Canada and said, 'It's tough to soar like an eagle when you're surrounded by two turkeys like Armand Pohan and the Ray Moron—I mean, Miron.' And I made little statements like, 'Ray Miron showed me a book with the title, *All I Know About Hockey*. And when I opened the book, the pages were blank.' Statements like that sealed my fate because no G.M. would hire me. After all, the fans loved me."

I saw this book when I was out in Colorado with my parents while searching for a house. The Mirons were kind enough to have the family over for dinner. They were quite proud of the book, and it amused them when they told us it had been a Christmas gift from the players. We all just shook our heads. Little did we know how true a gift it was.

Let's not forget that Dad's favourite Bruin was Stan Jonathan, a full-blooded Tuscarora, born in Ohsweken, a Six Nations reserve near Brantford, Ontario. When Stan was charged with criminal negligence in a hunting accident in 2012 (which was later withdrawn), Dad and I went to a fundraising event for his defence. However, Dad felt the ire of Stan's father. When Dad met him and said, "Your son reminds me of my dog," it didn't go over well. He obviously didn't know the love Dad had for his beloved Blue.

Another time Dad's attitude toward Indigenous peoples was questioned was when he and Ron got into a discussion about Chris Simon, who is of Ojibwe descent from the Wiikwemkoong First Nation. Simon got a thirty-game suspension for an attack on the Rangers' Ryan Hollweg in 2007, at the time one of the stiffest suspensions ever handed out by the NHL. Seeing that Simon was Ojibwe and Ron believed his suspension was unjust, Ron basically asked Dad if his upbringing could have affected why Simon felt he was being treated unfairly. Ron's thought process was, *A lot of First Nations kids go to bed at night and wake up in the morning thinking they won't get a fair shake. Until Chris accepts that he's being treated fairly, the message won't sink in.*

Dad said that the minute the words came out of his mouth, Ron knew he was in trouble. He saw the glint in Dad's eye, knowing that Dad had him: "What? You're saying that Natives have an inferiority complex when something happens to them?" Ron, probably knowing this was not a good subject to be treading on, tried to raise the point that sometimes Indigenous peoples are not treated fairly. Dad's response was viewed as racist: "Fair shake in life? Go out and get your own fair shake in life and work for it. Don't give me that stuff." Well, as Dad would say, the left-wingers had a field day with this. What nobody knows is that, soon after that statement, Dad got a phone call in support from a person high up in the Indigenous community, saying what Dad said was true. I wish I could tell you who it was, but I don't really know. I bet they're glad I don't. This person believed in tough love with no crutch, which is taboo to say in this day and age.

Dad also found out you could be called a racist for saying the most innocent, comical, and obvious thing. In 1989, he was asked about what he thought of the Winnipeg Jets' assistant coach, Alpo Suhonen, who is Finnish. Remembering that Mom fed Blue Alpo products, Dad replied, "Alpo? Isn't that a dog food?" The team's owner, Barry Shenkarow, called Dad a racist and threatened to sue him.

Nothing gets more of a response from reporters than when Dad does something outside of HNiC. In 2010, the newly elected mayor of Toronto Rob Ford asked Dad to put the chain of office around his neck at his inaugural council meeting. Dad was honoured, as the city clerk normally did this. This was announced about a week before the event, which gave the media time to comment on Ford's decision, and did they ever have a field day. They made fun of Dad for going to church, called him "maudlin" for continually honouring the Canadian troops on Coach's Corner, and on and on. At the time, the debate about all the bicycle lanes in Toronto and bicyclists' rights were in the news too. I, like a lot of people, have a problem with cyclists and their high and mighty attitudes. They want accolades for being so wonderful that they use a bike to get around, but most don't follow the rules of the road. When I used to walk my dog down in Port

Credit, Ontario, it wasn't the cars I worried about, but the maniacs on bikes. The really arrogant ones who dress in neon getups and tight bike shorts (think Cam on the old TV show *Modern Family*) constantly back up traffic. They bike in packs and take up a whole lane. To counteract this frustration, I am the person who stops at the traffic light and pulls over as close as I can to the curb so they can't fly through the light. I am just trying to look out for you. I won't even mention a person I know who extends his side mirror in his F-350 truck so you can't get by. Trust me, I know this is wrong, but you know they will get even, and when you have cars vs bikes, guess who is going to win?

Needless to say, Dad was gunning for bear when he went in and spoke for three minutes. He said he noticed that the downtown councillor, Adam Vaughan, had turned his back to him. The papers said he turned his back halfway through the speech because he was so enraged by Dad's comments. Whichever it was I'd say it's pretty rude, even if you disagree with what a speaker is saying. Afterwards Vaughan seemed to lighten up, saying, "For the record, I think Don Cherry's been in the shower with more naked left-wingers than I ever have," but he later added, "I think all of you in the press gallery deserve more respect. You're citizens of the city and you shouldn't be invited down to an event like this and castigated for political opinions which privately you're entitled to hold and professionally you don't." That's *castigated*, not castrated.

As Dad strolled up to the podium in what was described as a loud, neon-pink, flowery silk jacket, you knew he was in a bad mood. He started with, "I'm wearing pinko for all the pinkos out there that ride bicycles and everything—I thought I'd get it in." Some laughed, some clapped, and most moaned, as they knew what they were in for. He went on to say, "Waddya expect, Ron MacLean to come here?" He then explained that he was befuddled by criticism of Ford's choice of him.

"I'm being ripped to shreds by the left-wing pinko newspapers out there—it's unbelievable. One guy called me a jerk in a pink suit, so I thought I'd wear that for him today." He turned to Rob and said, "This is what you'll be facing, Rob, with these left-wing pinkos—they scrape the bottom of the barrel." He went on to praise Ford as "honest, he's truthful, he's like Julian Fantino—what you see is what you get," referring to the former OPP commissioner who had recently won a federal by-election in Vaughan for the Conservatives.

He ended his speech by telling the story of city staff cutting down a tree on the property of a 75-year-old Alzheimer's patient for no good reason, and stonewalling her son after the woman was given a $4800 bill. He went on to say, "Rob's in the mayor's office one day—an apology comes and a $5000 cheque, and that's why I say he's going to be the greatest mayor this city has ever seen." He ended with, "As far as I'm concerned, you can put that in your pipe, you left-wing kooks."

Rob, who laughed through all of Dad's speech, later said, "To each his own, right? Don's well known, he's well respected throughout Canada, and what you see is what you get." When he was asked if he knew his special guest was going to use his airtime to attack political opponents, he replied, "I didn't know. I've been a huge fan."

When Dad was leaving, he was told there was a side door to exit through so he wouldn't have to go out amongst the waiting crowd. There was no way Dad would let anyone think he was ducking out, so he walked straight through. Even the *Toronto Star*'s city hall reporter David Rider said afterwards it was hard for reporters seeking comments from him, as they had to fight through a long line of people seeking his autograph and photo. What was Dad's parting comment to those criticizing his speech? "Well, what can I tell you? Don't invite me. You don't invite a pit bull. If you want a pit bull, you get a pit bull." I guess he forgot they are banned in Ontario.

CHAPTER 6

MISOGYNIST?

D ad has been called many things. In one Coach's Corner, Ron held up a list of names that one newspaper had called him. My mom, Rose, once said in an interview, "They call him such terrible names that I have to look some of them up to see what they mean." The more amusing ones were "troglodyte," "pinhead," "moron," and "blather-mouth." But since this was the nineties, I am sure she had to look up "misogynist" and "xenophobic." What it does prove is how she had developed a thick skin when it came to people judging and commenting on her husband. Looking back, I realize it could have been very easy for her to be bitter towards these people who assumed so much about her husband. She was a person who lived in the reality of knowing that, if your husband is going to make a nice living out of giving his opinion on air, you better be prepared to suffer being judged and ridiculed. The adage of "if you dish it out, you'd better be prepared to take it" rang true regarding the man she loved. She knew this was the way it was, accepted it, and took it in stride. However, knowing how Dad really feels about women and that he is not a chauvinist, it takes a lot of self-discipline to not care what other people think.

She knew she was the boss in her household. Dad respected her opinion and heeded her recommendations. She controlled the money and raising the kids, and if anyone wanted Don for endorsements, speaking engagements, etc., they had to deal with Rose. Make no mistake about it: he was the soft one and Mom was the tough one. The organization Mothers Against Drunk Drivers wanted Dad to be the spokesperson for a campaign and Mom politely declined. After more discussion, they insinuated to Mom that Don didn't care about drunk driving. I walked in on the conversation just as she told them how she resented their comments and that they were way out of line. When I see their ads on TV now, I think about how Mom stood up to their high and mighty, untouchable attitude.

I believe nothing reflects a man's attitude toward women more than how they treat waitresses, whether it's at a bar, nightclub, or restaurant. I have seen how some men—especially when they are with Dad, for some reason—treat them. They will be condescending, with undertones of uncomfortable conversation, insinuations, and innuendos. He immediately calls them on it and tells them that, as long as they are in his company, they will treat the staff with the respect they deserve. Waitresses are hard-working, most earning minimum wage or less, and often they are single moms just trying to keep their heads above water in these challenging times. So, if you think they put up with you because of your good looks and charm, know that you are just being tolerated for your tips, or worse, fear of losing their job. Trust me, I have worked at enough bars, and our family has owned enough of them, to make that observation firsthand. Enough said about that.

When Dad was coaching, he always felt that the team, when in public, was a reflection of himself, since he was the man in charge. I said this to my toddler years ago: his behaviour in public was a reflection of me and my parenting skills. Your dog is also a reflection of you. Trust me, I'm a dog groomer: if you see a well-balanced, mannerly dog, chances are you'll like the owner.

The control Dad had over his team was well reflected when they travelled. Flight attendants have even come up to him and commented on how polite and respectful his team was compared to some professional athletes they had to deal with. Unfortunately, one player had to learn this the hard way after bugging an attendant. Dad warned the player (a goalie) to knock it off, but then he touched the attendant's behind. Dad jumped on top of him, put his hands around his throat, and choked him. He held him so hard that he said he hurt his thumbs. To this day, when he grabs something hard and squeezes, his thumbs ache and he curses this guy. Talk about setting the precedent for the next time he told a player to knock it off.

He was forever a fan of women's hockey thanks to his dear friend Hazel McCallion, the ex-mayor of Mississauga. She played on a professional women's hockey team in Montreal in the 1920s, and she and Mom encouraged Dad to tell the public that these women should be treated fairly in our national game. In 1997, the chairman of the Canadian Hockey Association, Bob MacKinnon, said, "The growing popularity of the women's game in our country owes a great deal to Don and Rose Cherry. They both supported the 1997 Women's World Hockey Championship in Kitchener, which was the most successful of the four world championships held so far. Don has been a strong supporter of the female game since the early 1980s and continues to speak out in favour of women's hockey. It's a pleasure for me, as chairman of Canadian Hockey, to be a part of this tribute to Rose Cherry, who was a keen supporter of female hockey herself."

The Canadian women's Olympic team wore a rose patch on their sweaters for their pre-Olympic games in memory of Mom, who passed away that year. November 7, 1997 was a special night, when Dad returned to Kitchener where he had played in the Eastern Professional Hockey League (EPHL) in 1960. At the Memorial Auditorium, with his grandson Del, he did the ceremonial puck drop between the U.S. and Canadian women's Olympic teams. When you witness this kind of tribute and respect, it's hard to believe that he has been accused of being a "person who has a hatred of, an aversion to, or is prejudiced against women," which is the definition of a misogynist, according to the Merriam-Webster dictionary.

Some would say, including my mother, that he brings such accusations upon himself. For instance, what began as Dad standing up for Duncan Keith became a controversy involving a female reporter that later turned into a debate about women reporters in males' dressing rooms. He addressed this on Coach's Corner, telling Ron: "I don't believe . . . women should be allowed in the male dressing room. I remember the first time it happened to me. Guys are walking around naked, and I hear this woman's voice and I turn around and there's a woman, and she's asking me about the power play, and I say, 'Let's go outside,' and she said, 'I'm not embarrassed,' and I said, '*I'm* embarrassed.'"

As expected, Ron disagreed with Dad's take and pointed out that any job should have equal opportunities for both men and women. Dad replied, "Then why aren't men in women's dressing rooms?" Ron's only rebuttal: "Well, why not?" Here is what Robin Herman, the first female reporter assigned to cover the NHL for the *New York Times* in the mid-seventies, said about Dad: "Don Cherry was the first coach of an NHL team to allow me into the locker room as a matter of policy. He was my hero. You were a stand-up guy."[7] Now this might sound like a contradiction, but as she would suggest, it's not like Dad would want women banned in the dressing room. The issue for him is the players' behaviour, not the women covering the game.

Andi Petrillo, who has been covering sports since 2006 and was a reporter for HNiC, said she wasn't offended by comments Dad made in 2013, saying, "I think his comments were misinterpreted, and if you actually listen to what he was saying, it wasn't so much about women not being in the dressing room as it was about players perhaps not conducting themselves appropriately around women." She later said that she and Dad frequently talk "legitimate hockey" and "if he was sexist, I don't think he would give me the time of day."[8]

Out of all this debate, I will tell you the one group that detests women in the dressing room more than any other: the wives. This discussion would often come up in the wives' room before games. In fact, a player came to Dad and said his wife did not like women in the dressing room. To try to make everyone happy, Dad let them have one-on-one interviews in his tiny office connected to the dressing room. Of course, the male reporters thought this was unfair to them. Needless to say, Dad was in a no-win situation.

Another comment he made about women that some took offence to was, "When you come to the games, keep your eyes on the puck. I'm telling ya, I've seen some awful smacks, and it's always a woman yapping away

[7]   Sturgeon, Jamie. "As Bruins Coach, Cherry Welcomed Women Reporters in Locker Room." *Global News*, 30 Apr. 2013, https://globalnews.ca/news/520194/as-bruins-coach-cherry-welcomed-women-into-locker-room/

[8]   Shah, Maryam: "Ron MacLean Defends Women Reporters and His Old School Pal." *Torontosun*, 29 Apr. 2013, https://torontosun.com/2013/04/28/don-cherry-catches-flak-for-locker-room-comment

there. Look at the game." I guess it's the delivery that causes offence, but his heart is always in the right place. He really wanted people to heed his warning about pucks going into the stands. We have sterilized the sport, and don't have to worry about it now that the stands behind the goals are covered in netting. This brings me to another point: why do some rinks have black netting that you have to look through, when the ice is white? Originally, the Air Canada Centre (now the Scotiabank Arena) had black netting, later switching over to white. Could it be because I complained to Dad how stupid this was, and as a season-ticket holder he had the right to complain? Never one to not give his opinion, he went ahead and expressed his discontent, though he never once sat in the seats he paid for. I'd like to think I had something to do with it (but I doubt it).

Though I don't like the netting and would prefer to take my chances at a game so I don't have to look through it, it does serve a purpose. Our season seats are the perfect place to watch a game. It's always on the curve, about two or three rows above the glass at the visitors' end, opposite the benches. This is where Mom and I sat for the teams Dad coached, the Boston Bruins and the AHL's Rochester Americans. That way you can see in every corner, have fun watching the benches, and hopefully see your team scoring in two periods.

Here is a tidbit that is hard to believe: Dad was at an event at the ACC when it was under construction as a favour to the Leaf management. They were putting in the seats then, so Dad thought it would be a good time to pick his season seats. Knowing the parameters described above, he picked out his spots. Out of 19,800 seats, he happened to pick seats promised to someone very special. The Leaf's management called him up and said, "We have a problem." Dad's reply was, "I don't, but you do."[9]

When I sat in those seats before the cautionary measures were in place, the first thing I did was to see if the goalie held his stick in his right hand. If he did, you knew he would clear it over the glass right at us to get the whistle. Plus, you had better pay attention during the warmups. I always like to watch them, especially at the visitors' end. I like to see the dynamics of it all. I like to watch to see if the goalie leaves the crease upset if the

---

[9]   Here's another funny tidbit. We had the same positioning of our seats at the old Maple Leaf Gardens. When we went to the opening game for the new ACC, we had the same usher, named Dave. What are the odds of that?

players are shooting high on him. As Dad always said, the warmup is only to warm the goalie up, not take his head off. This was never more evident when Dad was in New York coaching Rochester in the early seventies. We needed to win the game that night to make the playoffs. Dad let a rookie play that management was keen on. During the warmup his shot went high, and the goalie, Lynn Zimmerman, raised his hand to protect his head. Dad, who never watches warmups, was in his office, and the trainer, Nate Agnello, came in flustered. Dad just looked at him and knew. He even told him, "Let me guess: Zimmy's hurt and it was the rookie that did it."

Speaking of warmups, Dad had a hard time watching my son's team warm up. There is little doubt that when kids reach the age that they can raise the puck, they love to use the goalie as target practice, and Del played goal. You would think that the coaches would enlighten them, but nope, they're oblivious to this fact. Dad always tried to get there just as the puck dropped so he wouldn't have to watch the firing squad take shots at his grandson. I remember him saying, "I hope Del makes it through to the game." The coaches don't know. I'd even have to watch wannabe hockey-player dads on the ice go in and score on him for fun to show what an accurate and hard shot they had. I thought, *Isn't that great? Demoralize your goalie while you show off.* It was so painful to watch that most of the time you could find me in my car writing Christmas cards. After Christmas I'd work on Easter cards—time management is very important to me.

I could write a another book on being a hockey mom and witnessing these coaches and the goings-on in minor hockey. For instance, they make the kids do drill after drill after drill, with no scrimmages, all so the parents will be impressed with these progressive coaches and their intricate drills. These follies were so complicated that one time two coaches collided mid-ice while they were showing the kids what they wanted them to do, and one ended up with a broken leg. Unfortunately I missed it because I was writing my Christmas cards. I would have loved to have seen it. Perhaps it's good that I didn't, because I would have killed myself laughing. Everyone was horrified, but I thought it proved my point that the drills are too complicated.

So, getting back to our seats—sure, I know the value of the netting. In fact, one night my son and his dad came home with a game puck that was aimed directly at Del from a Stevie Thomas slapshot. His dad saw it coming, shielded him from getting hit, and took a nice kidney shot. It left a black rubber mark on his Maple Leafs sweater, which he was very proud of.

And yes, I am one of those people who talk throughout the game. There is a skill to it, believe it or not. I can talk and not miss a play. I could never figure out why people feel they have to look at you when they speak. Your voice doesn't get any clearer or louder if you are talking *at* me. Mom and I talked throughout whole games. She too didn't miss a thing, but she'd admit that she never saw an offside, because she never knew the rules of it. Icings she understood, but offsides: not a clue and she really didn't care. She said that's what they have referees for.

Once at the Boston Gardens when Dad was coaching the Bruins, Mom and I saw him going nuts over a call. Mom asked, "What is your father so upset about?" I had to explain that he didn't think it was offside. He had a thing about anyone going offside if Bobby Orr had the puck. When asked by players what the game plan was in this situation, he'd say, "Just stay onside." Do you blame him? Bobby would start on a roll and *boom*, there'd be a whistle. I really felt for the guy who went offside and had to take the skate of shame back to the bench. Dad was always waiting for him at the open gate with his hands on his hips. Even the fans knew, and when Dad would start chewing out their ears, Mom would say, "I think he's going a little overboard." I sure loved hockey in those days.

So yes, talking during a game is a God-given right. I went to a game with Leanne Domi once when we sat right behind the bench, and we talked through the whole game. Afterwards, we met up with Tie and he mentioned in his oh-so-nice way, "You two never shut up the whole game," which was true and we admitted it. Then we told him his mind should be on the game, not on us yapping.

Speaking of sitting behind the bench, I wish those people knew how much they are on TV. If any of them are *Seinfeld* fans who watched the episode where everyone made fun of George stuffing his face at a sporting event, they'd be more particular about eating the way they do. I love watching the people eating behind the bench, never gracefully. I was one of those people. I love popcorn at the game, and mix caramel corn with regular. I can make this combo last three periods, but there's no way I would do it while sitting behind the bench. I knew there would be someone like me watching and saying, "How long does it take that woman to eat a bag of popcorn?" One time I was there with a friend, sitting right behind the Leafs' spare goalie, James Reimer. My friend wanted something to eat and insisted I get some popcorn, but I settled for M&Ms because they can be eaten discreetly. Sure enough, just as he tucked into his huge slice of pizza, the Leafs got three quick goals scored on them. I knew they were showing the backup goalie on TV, thinking they were going to pull their starter. Sure enough, Reimer grabbed his glove, mask, and stick and took the ice, and the dejected goalie ended up sitting right in front of us. All the while I knew we are on TV, and many people later pointed out that they saw us. I was never so glad not to have popcorn as my friend, oblivious to this whole scenario, struggled to wolf down his huge slice of pizza—not pretty. This guy is a major player in the Domino's franchise, and the pizza he was wolfing down was by Pizza Pizza. I could never understand how he could eat his competitor's food on sheer principle, let alone while everyone was watching.

One has to look no further when evaluating someone's true character than observing them at work. One of Dad's most treasured relationships at HNiC was with the producer of Coach's Corner, Kathy Broderick. Here was a woman who rose through the ranks of the huge corporation of CBC/Rogers/Sportsnet. If ever there was a boys' club, the HNiC broadcasts would be it. Yet she survived and succeeded not because of her gender and others' tokenism, but by her wits and knowledge of the game. Dad recognized this and valued her as a colleague and friend. Yet she was no pushover with him.

I witnessed her setting him straight numerous times about why they couldn't do this or that during a broadcast. What I love about her most was how secure she was within herself. She didn't care if anyone saw her bringing Dad and Ron coffee and bran muffins while they were watching a morning skate on the road. They would sit far up from the ice, and one by one *real* hockey people would come to have a chat, then leave. If ever there was a time to hear real hockey commentating, that was it. But no one broke the trust, and it was all very respectful. She had an eye for hockey and knew what Dad wanted to show on Coach's Corner. She'd show a lot of the fun stuff to Dad, like things that went on at the bench or during warmups, to see if he wanted to mention it. I often told him that I wouldn't praise her too much in public about how much she knew about hockey, because being lumped in with him might be a career-limiting move.

Another person he really admired and respected was the makeup artist for HNiC/CBC. He treated her with the utmost respect and friendship for the great work she did. I can't say that for everyone on HNiC or the CBC who she did makeup for.

I was looking at Tim's birdfeeder in his backyard one day, and what I at first thought was an overgrown goldfinch turned out to be a yellow parakeet that had obviously gotten loose. Knowing it wouldn't last over the winter, we caught it. With no owner to be found, Dad went out and bought a cage with all the bells and whistles and brought it down to CBC on a Saturday to give to the makeup stylist. It must have been quite the sight to see Don Cherry getting out of his limo and walking into the CBC studios with this birdcage. That's how much he thought of her.

Another time he wanted her as an extra for an opening he was doing outside during the playoffs. She didn't show up and he asked her why. She explained that a new hire wanted his makeup done early, and had said in so many words that her job was to do his makeup, not be some extra for Don Cherry. When Dad heard this, he confronted the guy and enlightened him that he hadn't been there very long, and that he'd better learn his place. Dad had a way of making a level playing field for all.

He told me a story about an incident that only my dad would have an issue with. He came to the makeup chair to find freshly cut hair on the floor. He was aghast. I guess the "stars" have the option of getting their hair cut before the show. Dad could see this was hair from several of the hired help and, I know this seems trivial, but it just grossed him out. Needless to say, the floors were swept clean when he was around after that.

He also had a problem with the stars not drinking the coffee that was made for them at the studio. Once a bunch of them wanted Starbucks, and it just so happened that Del was the coffee gofer that day. I told him, "Don't let Granddad see you leaving the building when you are doing your Starbucks run." Sure enough, Dad saw him in the halls and asked him where he was going, and my son, who would not lie, told him. Well, doesn't he go into a tirade about how the coffee is "good enough for me but not for all these stars who need their expensive coffee," and on and on.

Some may think it was because his grandson was the one being sent for the coffee, but that was not the case. There have been many executives of HNiC who started out as runners.

You can only imagine how frustrating it was for my mother to see how the press portrayed him as a misogynist. Sure, he brought it on himself, and that's how she rationalized it, but remember this quote he said in defence of himself on Coach's Corner: "I don't feel women are equal. I feel they're above us. I think they're on a pedestal and they should not be walking in when naked guys are walking around. And you know some guys take advantage of it, and I don't think it should be allowed."

One thing is for sure: he had her way up on that pedestal.

CHAPTER 7

THE FRENCH

D ad has certainly had Francophones in Canada consistently upset with him throughout the years. If they only knew the respect he has for them, even though what he's said has sometimes rattled their chains. Some comments even prompted an investigation from the Official Language Commissioner, and even Quebec's MP, Vincent Della Noce, called for the House of Commons to censure Cherry for "taking a malicious pleasure in ridiculing Francophones by saying the people of Sault Ste. Marie speak the 'good language.'" I personally don't remember him saying that, but you never know. Francophones being upset with him goes way back to 1991, when Eric Lindros said before the NHL draft that he would prefer not to play for the Quebec Nordiques. The French crucified this eighteen-year-old kid, calling him a racist and a musclebound Ontarian. The Nordiques wouldn't trade him, even though Eric said he would play in Montreal. But as Dad explained to Ron on Coach's Corner, Eric knew there was no way they would trade him to their all-time rivals, the Habs, who were in their division. If you go back and watch this Coach's Corner segment, it is enlightening and Dad makes some logical points. Knowing that Eric wouldn't sign with them, the Nordiques could have gotten a lot for him and would have had a shot to beat out the Hartford Whalers in the tough Adams Division for a playoff spot.[10] To this, Ron replied, "Yeah, but they might have won the Stanley Cup with Eric."

---

[10] FYI: they ended up in last place.

I might mention here that Dad had many nicknames for Ron, and one was "Yeah But," his rebuttal to many of Dad's comments. The other one was "TOG." I never realized how true this was until I noticed people saying the same thing to me when trying to remember Ron's name: "You know, that other guy," so TOG it was. Dad then explained why a rookie would want to go to Quebec, and used Joe Sakic as an example. Here was a player who had three seasons with over a hundred points, plus he was in the running for Rookie of the Year, and hardly anyone had heard of him. He ended up having no endorsement opportunities while playing seven seasons in Quebec. Let's face it, most of us remember him only playing for Colorado. That was the reality, whether people believed it or didn't want to hear the truth. This was a lively segment, and if you go back to watch it, it was the first time I noticed Dad pounding his fingers on the HNiC desk. I wasn't the only one to see this habit: there is a YouTube video of Dad playing the piano on Coach's Corner that is worth watching. The added piano sound is right on to the chords being struck. Not only that, but his red velvet suit with the Santa Claus tie is stunning.

The backstory on this is amusing. Many people sent us the link to this two-minute video. We loved it so much that my brother decided to put it on a *Rock'em Sock'em* video. He found out who did it, a young kid. Knowing you should ask for permission before using it, he called the family up. The mother answered and told her son that the Cherry family was calling. I guess the kid got scared thinking we were angry and accused his friend of posting it. He was relieved when we told him we wanted to honour his work by putting it on *Rock'em Sock'em*. It's very amusing to watch and I enjoy it to this day.

I believe there were issues that Dad would bring to light not only because of his true feelings, but because they were paths that politicians and the press would fear to tread. For instance, no one responded to the Bloc Quebecois party members complaining that there were too many Canadian flags in the Olympic Village during the 2008 Olympics in Nagano, Japan. You know Don Cherry had something to say about that. I believe his response reflected what many people were thinking, but in true style they wouldn't utter such words out of fear of being accused of being racist, anti-French . . . pick your poison. So, what's Dad's rebuttal on Coach's Corner? "So, they don't like the Canadian flag. You know, it's funny, they don't want the flag, but they want our money." He also figured political correctness and politics had a part in picking the flag-bearer that year in the Olympics, saying, "Then we pick a French guy, some ski guy that nobody knows about." Which, again, is probably true, for how many Canadians had ever heard of Jean-Luc Brassard? (Picard, maybe, but not Brassard). Needless to say, he really got ripped for these comments.

Dad admitted to the press, "I knew I'd get in a little trouble, but I didn't think I'd get in the House of Parliament." The topic of players wearing visors started on *Grapeline*, his radio talk show with Brian Williams, in 2004. He was quoted as saying, "Usually the guys who are cutting players are the ones who wear visors . . . because they don't show the same respect as those who do not." The point he was trying to make made sense if you knew the culture of hockey. When no one wore visors, there was a code of respecting one another's safety. When players feel invincible, their game strategy changes. Sticks start coming up, habits are formed, and there you have it, more injuries, and the players without visors are labelled stupid for not protecting themselves with face shields. On Coach's Corner, he was addressing his comments made on his radio show referring to players who wore visors as "mostly Europeans and French guys." This incensed French Canadian interest groups, CBC executives, and federal Members of Parliament. It even prompted investigations from the CBC ombudsman, the Canadian Broadcast Standards Council, and Dyane Adam, the official language commissioner. She agreed to investigate whether Dad had violated the Official Languages Act when the Canadian Parents for French organization filed a formal complaint with the CBC. Who would have guessed that such a group existed?

I watched the CBC news that night and saw the interview with the father who had initiated this complaint. It was amusing to see his interpretation of Dad's quotes, saying that he called visor-wearing players "cowards." Interpretation is everything. When one extrapolates to their version, that is where quotes, facts, and gullibility merge and the waters become muddy. Just an FYI in defence of Dad: a Winnipeg lawyer, Curtis Unfried, told CBC Newsworld that 59 percent of European players and 55 percent of Quebec players wear visors, while just 20 percent of North Americans born outside of Quebec wear them (remember, the year is 2004). After that came out, the *Toronto Star* printed their stats regarding visors along with the *Canadian Press,* showing that Dad was correct in his "assumption." In true style, the CBC denounced Dad's opinion (that they pay him handsomely to deliver) and supposedly put a seven-second delay on Coach's Corner to appease the grumbling. This makes you think about future "controversies" that may have arisen that weren't averted. Was there really a delay, or did they just say that to appease the whiners? We will never know.

I opened this chapter by saying the French don't realize how much he admires them. They fight for what they believe in. If they think their language is not being represented enough throughout Canada, they do something about it. They consider themselves unique beyond the rest of Canada and value their traditions. When a group comes to Quebec and forces their traditions upon them, they speak out. It's admirable, and I wish the rest of Canada let their ideals be known as the French do. I have always found it amazing how many people would say to our family that our father only says what the rest of them think. I find that sad but true.

On a personal level, Dad had many French players he considered special friends. You have to look no further than defenceman Carol Vadnais, who was with the Bruins when Dad got there. It was Vadnais who replaced the glass stones in Dad's Calder Cup ring with real diamonds. He was also the one who explained to Dad that the buttonholes on the cloth napkins in first class on a plane were meant to be attached to your shirt during mealtime. Once, they were out to dinner in a classy restaurant. Carol knew how to order fancy wine and such, but he made sure not to make Dad feel inadequate, asking the waiter for some ketchup for Dad's steak. Now that is a friend.

He considered Carol one of his best friends back then. He was quoted in 2013 as saying, "Don's a great guy. All that stuff he says about Quebecers he says to get people riled. He's a good coach and a good friend." Spoken like a secure and confident person. So, what happens after Dad gets to Boston? His best friend is traded to the New York Rangers along with Phil Esposito in exchange for Brad Park, Joe Zanussi, and another French gentleman, Jean Ratelle. Dad used to say Jean was such a classy guy that when Dad went off on one of his hockey rants, using F-bombs like candy, he'd look over at Jean and feel embarrassed. He treated him like a veteran player should be treated: with loving care and respect.

On one particular flight, he knew Jean would appreciate the great food and wine first class had to offer. Dad was never one to eat or drink on a flight; he'd wait to eat the sandwiches packed in his suitcase. As he knew the perks of first class would be wasted on him, he went back to where Jean was sitting with Bobby Schmautz. He told Jean that he wanted to talk to Bobby, and to go up and sit in his seat. Jean did not want to go, but Dad insisted. When Jean left, Bobby asked what he wanted to talk to him about, not knowing he was rewarding his veteran player for his contribution to the team. I'm sure Mr. Ratelle knew what the buttonhole on his napkin was for.

Here's a Ratelle story for the books: Schmautzy adding fuel to the fire regarding the relationship between Bruins' GM Harry Sinden and Dad. Believe it or not, Harry gave a note to Dad telling him not to play Ratelle against Montreal right before the game, saying he didn't play well against them. Dad gave it to Schmautzy, who of course showed it to Ratelle. Not only did Dad play him, but Ratelle scored a hat trick. To inflame the relationship even more, he waved to Harry up in his box, where he was sitting with the owners. I often wondered what he would've said if one of those owners asked, "Why is Don waving to you?" When you ask Dad what he was thinking, all he says is, "I must have been nuts."

Another good friend of Dad's was Rene Robert, best known for being one-third of the French Connection, the line consisting of Rene, Gilbert Perreault, and Rick Martin that reigned in Buffalo from 1972 to 1979. Rene also played for Dad on the Colorado Rockies in 1979–80, and scored 28 goals with 35 assists. It's there that they became good friends and kept up their friendship long after hockey was a thing of the past for each. He routinely came over to the house in Mississauga, where Blue welcomed him with many kisses. She wasn't the most affectionate dog, so Mom and I would always say to him that it was his aftershave Blue liked.

One day he brought friends over, and they wanted to meet the famous Blue. Unfortunately, no one told Rene that Blue did not respond to finger-snapping as a command. Calling her is OK, but there was no way she'd come if you snapped your fingers. Needless to say, Blue didn't run over to see her friend as eagerly as she usually would, and Rene never figured out why.

Mom and I always said that when the French Connection was in its prime, Rick Martin looked like a movie star, by far the best-looking of the three. Remember, in those days players wore no helmets, and to see their flowing hair and perfectly chiselled features really added to the game's entertainment value. Needless to say, Dad couldn't wait to tell Rene and embarrass us. Rene acted hurt, but he retained his own movie-star good looks even after retirement. The Cherry family was stunned when he passed away in a Florida hospital in 2021, less than a week after suffering a heart attack. He was only 72 years old.

Through all the controversies, it was often said that Dad would say these things to get a rise out of people, and that it was his way of getting in the spotlight and causing a debate. I hate to say it, folks, but it is none of this—he just speaks his mind. He truly has no malice. For instance, in 2006 the NY Islanders' winger Zigmund Palffy scored against the New Jersey Devils, and he celebrated by kissing teammate Travis Green on the lips. What was Dad's reaction? "I know those guys who wear visors are sweeties, but that's a little much." You can only imagine how many activists that comment upset. He just thought it was a humorous thing to say. In fact, in one of his *Rock'em Sock'em* tapes, he has a segment showing players kissing in celebration. So kissing isn't a big thing for Dad. Who can forget him kissing Doug Gilmour at least three times? One was in 1993, just after the first game of the Toronto-Los Angeles series to decide the Campbell Conference champs, plus when Doug's number was honoured by the Leafs, both on the HNiC set and once in the stands. He was forever giving Bobby Orr a kiss on camera, which came to be known as "giving him the Gilmour." He also kissed Nazem Kadri with glee after an Ottawa Senators game when he got a hat trick. The point should be made here that Kadri, whose father immigrated to Canada with his parents in the sixties, is one of the few players who commented non-negatively about Dad's controversial Poppygate issue. He was quoted as saying, "I know Grapes, and I don't think it came across like everyone is making it sound. I think with what he said, it was maybe just said incorrectly. People maybe took it out of context a little bit. I know Grapes is a great person and I'm sad to see him go." We understood that a lot of players had to tread lightly in what they said to the press about Poppygate. One wrong step in sticking up for Dad and they would be labelled racist, xenophobic etc. So Nazem's comments were greatly appreciated.

In ending this discussion concerning Dad's feelings toward the French and the allegations of xenophobia, I will finish by telling this little story about him enlightening me concerning people who speak a different language. I was complaining to Dad about a phone call I had with a customer-service representative with a heavy accent. Though I try hard not to be rude by saying, "Pardon? Please speak slower. Can you repeat that?" it does get frustrating. So, I was ranting and raving to Dad about why companies put people with English as their second or third language on the phone lines. I guess he was sick of listening to me and quickly shut me up by saying, "Remember, Cindy, those people can speak one more language than you."

That brought me into reality and shut me up fast. I never learned French in school, even though I was forced to take it in junior high in Rochester, New York. I could never understand if something was masculine or feminine, as in *le* and *la*. I remember arguing with my French teacher, Mrs. Follet, on how I should know if a door is masculine or feminine, which she explained alters the rest of the sentence. I then learned my go-to answer for when she'd ask me a question: "Je ne sais pas." I guess this was not a smart thing to do, but back then I'd never have guessed I would live in Canada for most of my adult life. Go figure that!

CHAPTER 8

MORE HOT WATER

D ad didn't need just Coach's Corner to get himself into hot water. There were other pulpits he could express himself quite well from. Whether they were public outings, TV commercials, or press interviews and articles, none had a premeditated agenda to upset people. He's been accused of saying outrageous things for the sake of getting a rise out of the public. Some may say it's in his marketing strategy, but trust me, this is not true. Here are just a few of these stories that really were innocently said.

Who knew a sports lottery commercial could get Dad in trouble and hurt feelings? When it aired in 1990, it featured him saying, "Come on, what do you think this is, a ballet practice?" Plus, "Don't forget to give those skates back to your sister, kid." This had unexpected consequences.

Taking umbrage at the snub to his profession, ballet instructor Bruce Monk, a former amateur hockey player, challenged Dad to see if he could keep up during an actual ballet practice. He also wanted to show Dad the training parallels between hockey and ballet. So, Dad became a special guest of the Royal Winnipeg Ballet, the longest continuously operating ballet company in North America. He entered a real ballet class, saying, "They tell me there are no fat guys in ballet, so I'm finished."

He was led through a series of stretches and leaps to the HNiC theme song with a young boy named Michael. He still found a way to work in some more humour by stating, "I'm starting to think I'm Tomas Sandström here!" At the end he took a bow and shook Michael's hand. Michael then handed him a pair of ballet slippers, saying, "Here's something to give back to *your* sister." It was all in good fun, with Dad admitting the dancers were all in great shape. Plus, he added that "the top guy gets only $19,000, and that's the way hockey players used to be." It was aired on HNiC and his point was made. Afterward, he got a wonderful thank-you letter from the ballet company, saying they appreciated the publicity that he gave them.

Some people have asked me how much of Coach's Corner was spontaneous. I'd say about 99 percent of it. Sure, Ron and Dad may have talked on Saturday mornings about what topics should be touched upon, but no one could rehearse the banter between those two. For instance, the discussion about seal burgers—who knew it would spark a controversy that would make the national news?

It all started when Ron was in St. John's, Newfoundland and Labrador, for a Rogers Hometown Hockey event in 2015, eating lunch at Mallard Cottage. He told Dad (who was in Toronto), "Guess what I had for lunch today?" Dad responded, "I know, I heard—you're eating a seal. A little baby seal. What are you, a savage? A barbarian?"

Ron quipped back, "I had a seal burger, and the only challenge for Chef Todd Perrin was that it was hard to know when to flip'er." Dad didn't take his flippancy too well, and as Ron was trying to find a segue into discussing the Leafs, Dad threw one more comment in to seal (pardon the pun) his fate. "Imagine eating a seal. What kind of barbarian . . ."

Well, these observations hit the airwaves in every form. It not only landed on social media, but the national TV news. Reps from Indigenous peoples, the politicians, and even the owner of the Mallard Cottage chimed in on this one. If you watched this restauranteur's interview on national TV, it looked like he was really working at keeping the smile off his face. He couldn't have bought the publicity he got from such exposure.

Matthew Coon Come, the national Chief of the Assembly of First Nations from 2000 to 2003, said, "According to Don Cherry, my Inuk friends are savages because they eat seal. The network should fire him for his racist remark.[11]

Plus we had Terry Audla, the president of the of national Inuit group Inuit Tapiriit Kanatam, go on CTV News and chime in on the subject.

---

[11]   CBC News: "Don Cherry Explains 'barbarian' Comment, Has 'no Problem' With Seal Meat." *CBC*, 8 Feb. 2015, https://www.cbc.ca/news/canada/newfoundland-labrador/don-cherry-explains-barbarian-comment-has-no-problem-with-seal-meat-1.2949490

He came off pretty good and intelligent by utilizing this opportunity to educate people about the importance of seals to his people, rather than just bashing Dad. He also brought up a good point by contrasting what his people do in harvesting seals versus industrial agriculture, which in his estimation is environmentally repugnant. He used his airtime well to get his points across, and for that I bet deep down he was appreciative of the controversy that Dad stirred up. As with the Winnipeg Royal Ballet Company, any airtime is good airtime.

Then, of course, you have the politicians looking to get their shining glory with their two cents. St. John's city councillor Tom Hann said, "Well, Don Cherry, barbarians, are we? Shows your ignorance, lack of knowledge, insensitivity!"[12]

Even the province's premier at the time, Paul Davis, chimed in, calling for Dad to apologize for what he thought was "insulting to Newfoundlanders and Labradorians."[13]

Environment minister Leona Aglukkaq had this to say: "Sealing is important to Inuit culture and tradition. Mr. Cherry's comments last night were hurtful and insensitive. I hope he apologizes. Our government will continue to defend Canada's humane seal hunt, which is so important to many of our northern and coastal communities."

The burger chef said the controversy over seal hunting was nothing new to Newfoundlanders as he was interviewed on CTV news the day after: "It's par for the course." He called Dad's choice of words "unfortunate," and stressed that his restaurant does not serve meat from "baby" seals. He went on to say that eating seal is commonplace in Newfoundland and Labrador and other parts of Northern Canada. "It's part of our culture," he said. "It's no different than eating a deer."[14]

---

[12] The Canadian Press. "Don Cherry Stokes Furor on Social Media With Seal Meat Comments." The Globe And Mail, 9 Feb. 2015, https://www.theglobeandmail.com/sports/hockey/don-cherry-stokes-furor-on-social-media-with-seal-meat-comments/article22853890/

[13] Rogers, Sarah: "Hockey Motor-mouth Don Cherry's 'Barbarian' Remark Ignites Seal Meat Furor." Nunatsiaq News, https://nunatsiaq.com/stories/article/65674seal_meat_eaters_barbarian_says_hockey_commentator/

[14] CTV News, "Don Cherry Responds to 'seal Burger' Controversy." CTVNews, 9 Feb. 2015 https://www.ctvnews.ca/canada/don-cherry-responds-to-seal-burger-controversy-1.2226216#

He added that he was surprised by the attention he received after Dad's comments, and "we certainly weren't expecting this type of reaction when Ron mentioned it on the show."

Now, Dad did come back and address the whole situation via Twitter, but made sure no one assumed he was doing it under pressure.

"Evidently, I upset some people about my seal burger comments. I would like to try to explain my comments. Not because I was told to or forced to, I do it because I feel I have hurt the feelings of some people I like and admire. I have friends who hunt deer and ducks, and I myself have eaten venison and duck meat. Just the same as people who hunt seals and eat seal meat. I have no problem with my friends who are hunters and eat venison and duck. Just the same as I have no problem with people who hunt seals and eat seal meat. I do, however, find it very unusual in my world that a person would go into a restaurant and order a seal burger for lunch. I meant no disrespect to the hunters who hunt and eat seal meat, just like I have no disrespect for the hunters who hunt deer and duck and eat their meat. Again, I do this explanation because I want to. I have hurt some people's feelings that I like and admire. If this explanation isn't good enough, then let the cards fall where they may."

I would like to point out that he mentioned having friends and even a relative who has hunted; he himself has never killed for hunger or sport. He understands all the rationalizations that hunters put forth, like a lot of people eat what they kill (or they will starve?). It's hard to believe that's true in Canada, but that's what I'm told. Some do it in the name of "conservation," the theory being that it is better they kill it than let it starve to death due to overpopulation, such as with deer. Plus, their hunting fees preserve wetlands (let's hope so).

Then there are the people who we shouldn't question about hunting because it's their God-given right to do so according to their culture and heritage. I can't debate that one. There are the exterminators that clear nature of "vermin," a great category to justify killing animals, for its distinction is all in the eye of the beholder. The definition of vermin is "wild animals that are believed to be harmful to crops, farm animals, and game, or that carry disease." You know what they say: it's all in the interpretation. Another category is the trophy hunters. They are probably the most honest, as there is no questioning why they kill: it's prestigious and they enjoy the thrill of the kill, and they make no bones about it.

My point is this: Dad never hunted and couldn't and wouldn't, unless you count fishing, which he hasn't done in a while. I used to fish myself, and looking back I wish I hadn't, even though some of my best times with my dad were spent fishing.

Dr. David Suzuki was once called the "Don Cherry of Canadian science,"[15] even though Dad only thought of him as "Chicken Little." He once appeared in a clip from Vancouver during a Coach's Corner segment, as Ron told Dad, "We have something for you from a pal of yours." Mr. Suzuki introduced himself as Don Cherry's favourite left-wing kook and explained that winter-sports fans know something strange was happening with weather and climate. He proceeded to ask sports fans to show their concern in the symbolic gesture of turning off our lights during Earth Hour, and ended by recommending that viewers keep their TV on to finish the game.

Ron came back knowing Dad was chomping at the bit to address this request, and asked Dad, "See how nice he was?"

Well, Dad addressed this request directly into the camera. "David Suzuki, left-wing kook, you're in Vancouver. It's warm out there. Why don't you come to Toronto? We've been freezing for two months . . . what is this 'warming trends'? We're all dying of cold, and he's talking warming trends."

It was all said in good fun, and quite the departure from the usual Coach's Corner.

Years later Dad and Ron were boarding a plane, and guess who was already sitting on board? Dad jokingly said, "Hey Ron, it's the guy who wants me to get rid of my Lincoln Mark VI." Mr. Suzuki made the point, "I don't care if you have it, just don't drive it." Years ago, I got a kick out of an article with the headline: DAVID SUZUKI HAS BECOME THE DON CHERRY OF TV SCIENCE. It described him as having a white beard and bully pulpit on CBC television, and evolved from geneticist to TV celebrity to his current role as the Don Cherry of Canadian Science, an angry curmudgeon lashing out at his enemies. Hmm . . . you could take that a few ways.

---

15   Fletcher, Tom. "B.C. VIEWS: David Suzuki Has Become The Don Cherry of TV Science." Terrace Standard, 8 Apr. 2019, https://www.terracestandard.com/opinion/b-c-views-david-suzuki-has-become-the-don-cherry-of-tv-science-6037570

The crown, straight from the Stratford
Shakespearean Festival

Brian Kilrea, Bob Orr, Dad at a Prospect Game practice

My inspiration in starting up a pet rescue foundation, Lucy.

Good times with the Cherry clan & Ron MacLean

Dad & Ron freezing at one of the many outdoor NHL winter games

A rare Don & Ron bobblehead produced to
promote organ donation in Canada

Del on the HNIC set with Grandpa & Ron

A table full of bobbleheads, a sight you won't see too often

Happy times with Dad, Tim, me & Ron

Dad, me & Tie Domi at one of the first Molson Indies in Toronto.

Dad and one of his favorite Pitbull players, Stan Jonathan

The power behind the throne

Hurricane Hazel who served as mayor from 1978-2014 & Dad
at the opening of the Rose Cherry's Home for Kids.

Two powerhouse woman behind the early days of women's
hockey, Fran Ryder & Hazel McCallion with Del

Grandson & Grandpa

Bobby Orr & me at a taping of the Grapevine
Show in Hamilton, Ontario

Carol Vadnais & me: no doubt the photographer was definitely a Bruin fan

Mike Walton (Lft) who played with Dad on the 65/66 Calder
Cup champs in Rochester & Rene Robert (Rt)

Fun times at a taping of the Grapevine TV Show in Hamilton, Ontario

March 31st, 1956

Mom with sister Paulette in Broken Arrow, Oklahoma

Dad was 22 & Mom 21 when they started their 41-year journey together

Summer of 1957 in Kingston, Ontario

My maternal grandmother, Mary Martini & Benji

Labrador Retriever, Dudgeon @ 8 weeks old

Dad & his beloved Dudgeon at 518 Albert Street in Kingston

Anna & grand-daughter @ Picton Beach, where I learned how to swim

Dad's grandmother Margaret Palamountain, her daughter Maudie and me

Dad's father & my son's namesake, Delmar Cherry

Mom's parents, John & Mary Martini, Hershey, Pa.

PART 2
A LIFE WELL LIVED

CHAPTER 9

THE LOVE STORY BEGINS

When the movie *Keep Your Head Up, Kid: The Don Cherry Story* came out in 2010, it was amazing how many men said that their wives loved the movie. At first glance you may have thought of it as a sports movie, but those who watched it said it was more of a love story. So it is with much pleasure that I can tell you how the Don and Rose story came about.

Mom was born and raised in Hershey, Pennsylvania—yes, where the chocolate bars are produced. Her father and mother worked in Milton Hershey's factory. As a little girl, I would take the factory tour and watch my grandmother pick up six candy bars at a time and put them in a box. That was the life of a factory worker back then: doing the same thing for eight hours straight.

Hershey was mainly an Italian town, so the Martinis—my mom's family—fit in well. As with most Italian families, they had loving nicknames for each other. My mother's went from Rosemarie Madalyn Martini to Tootsie Martini. Tootsie had a younger sister, Paulette, whom I thought of as a sister when I was growing up. As with most people in Hershey, Mom had a job at the factory and her career choice was to be a tour guide. Dad often told us the story of getting a guided tour of the factory with some of his fellow hockey players by a woman he had taken a shine to. To know how they met, you must meet her Aunt Ann Martini, a.k.a. Honey. Now here was a woman ahead of her time. She was married to my mom's uncle, Big Johnny, who was about five-seven. I think it was more his width than his height that got him that name. They owned a motel and bar called—what else—Martini's. Now, this bar was known throughout the hockey world. This is where all the American Hockey League teams went when they played against the Hershey Bears. Most players started out in this league, and if they were talented enough they'd go to the only six available teams in the NHL. Towards the twilight of their careers, they would usually end up back in the AHL. There were also five other pro leagues, all of which Dad played in, except the Quebec Hockey League.

Honey ran the business, and if you know the bar and motel world you know you have to be tough, and tough she was. She stood out from all the other Italian women in Hershey. She had a sinewy build, tall and lanky with her hair cut short, and she was loud and opinionated. To acknowledge this in a household of Italians is extreme. Even her cooking was different. When Big Johnny died, my grandmother said, "It was her cooking that killed him." I later asked my mom what Grandma meant, and all she said was, "It was all the fat in her food," and we all know how Italians cook. The most memorable trait Aunt Honey had was her flaring nostrils. When she came to visit, she would run to me and pinch my cheeks very hard. It got to the point where I would lock myself in the bathroom to prevent her loving pinches. One day I asked my grandma, "Why is Aunt Honey so different from the rest of us?" She whispered, "Because she is Serbian." I didn't know what that meant, but she said it like that was all she needed to say to explain everything. As an adult I asked her why the Serbians and Croatians are always at war. She answered matter-of-factly, "They've hated each other for so long they have forgotten why." She was quick-witted and tough as nails, and no one messed with her. Even the relatives treaded lightly around her.

She had a lot of trouble with my grandmother concerning me. Aunt Honey would take me to the bar in the mornings to help clean up. I was only about four or five years old. I remember loving its smell of old cigarettes and stale beer. It was one of those bars you would never want to see in the daylight, but I loved it. I had a particular job, but when I accidentally told my grandmother what I was doing she blew her stack, and that was the end of my bar visits. Aunt Honey had me clean the gum from under the tables. She motivated me to do a good job by promising me that if I found any shiny objects like rings stuck in the gum, I'd get a quarter. I thought this was great. My mom shook her head, but it was another reason for my grandmother not to be a big fan of hers.

Aunt Honey knew my dad, as he played for the Hershey Bears. She saw the quality in him. He stood out with his manners, always very polite. More importantly, he was no "hound dog." It was she who said to Dad, "You have to meet my niece." When I look back, she sure took a chance setting up a relative with a big, tough hockey player. The game plan was for him and a teammate to take a Hershey factory tour when Mom was working as the guide. After that, they dated throughout the season. Mom had never been to a hockey game, and the first one she saw that Dad played in there was a real donnybrook of a fight. Though she was sweet and innocent, I guess she liked what she saw.

To continue dating, Dad had to meet her parents. She stayed home and cooked dinner with her mom, and her new beau was to come over for dinner after the game. He showed up with a black eye and stitches from a fight to meet this meek and mild Italian family. Nonetheless, with his charm, manners, and respect for my mom, Mary and John Martini gave him the green light to continue dating their daughter. Then came the end of the season, and what else do the hockey players do but go home to Canada. Mom said she was fully prepared not to see or hear from him again. Love-struck, he returned home to Kingston, Ontario.

Missing the first love of his life over the summer, he couldn't stand it any longer. He went down to Kinnear d'Esterre jewellery store on Princess Street, bought a ring (that I wear today), then drove overnight down to Hershey. He got there early in the morning, so he slept in his car until a decent hour before knocking on their door. Mom answered with curlers in her hair, as she was getting ready for work. She opened the jewellery box, and he asked her to marry him. With no hesitation she said yes. I later asked her how she knew he was for her within such a short romance. All she said was, "You just know."

Her love for him was tested early on. Dad had no problem getting married in Hershey the following spring. However, it was to be in an Anglican church. I was surprised there was one in Hershey at the time. In those days, to renounce your Catholicism to become Protestant was beyond words. Her family was behind her and supported the decision; however, the priest, who had known her since she was a baby, announced in his sermon the Sunday before her wedding day that anyone attending this wedding would be excommunicated. Nice, eh? I never asked her who showed up, because I didn't want to know. I do know that none of Dad's family made it down to Hershey, and in true WASP fashion, it was never discussed why.

For years, my dad and his mom would go at it about the wedding announcement in Kingston's *Whig Standard.* To her dying day, my grandmother says it was a typo when the paper forgot the last "i" in Martini. Knowing how my grandmother felt about the "RCs," as she called them, I think Dad was right. When I asked her about it, my mother's feelings were, "Who cares?" Typo or not, it wouldn't have bothered her in the least. Dad? He blew his stack. Mom always said, "Why would you let things like that bother you?" I guess to survive with my dad all those years she had to live by that philosophy. Unfortunately I never inherited that trait, but my brother did. I wish I had that gene, for I believe life is much easier for those who let things slide. Mom and I constantly debated this philosophy.

For instance, I remember one dandy argument about Eric Lindros's mother, Bonnie, calling for Dad. I came in one day at the end of a conversation with Bonnie as Mom was saying, "You'll have to call back," and hung up. I knew she had called several times before, and I asked Mom why she didn't take her number so Dad could call her back. Mom nonchalantly replied that she didn't want to give out her number. I used the line Dad uses when he is ticked off: "Let me get this straight: she has your home number but you can't have hers?" Once again I got the old, "Why do you let things like that bother you?" She was mostly annoyed that Bonnie tended to call around 4:30 when *The Young and the Restless* was about to come on.

Here is another example of me being perturbed and my mother not caring less. A business associate was organizing our restaurant's charity golf tournament for the Kidney Foundation of Canada. She told Mom and me over lunch how she had bought all the prizes and raffle items at Canadian Tire. We are talking about twenty to thirty thousand dollars' worth of TVs, BBQs, bikes, tires—you name it, we had it.

Fast-forward to Christmas, and again we are having lunch discussing whether we had finished all our Christmas shopping. She proudly says she is all caught up, and that she had bought all her gifts with Canadian Tire money. I don't know if I was angrier that she thought we were stupid enough not to realize where all that Canadian Tire money came from, or that she used it for herself. Again, I have a problem with this, and good ol' Mom says I will get old before my time if I let stuff like that bother me. I know this and so does my dad, but we can't help it. If you know the fable of the scorpion and the frog, we are definitely scorpions—stinging is in our natures. We know when things don't make sense, but we can't help ourselves.

My mom and paternal grandmother were very much alike. They had to be to get along with my dad and raise me. For instance, one doozy of a row between my dad and his mom came from me opening my big yap as a five-year-old. I loved walking with my grandmother to the bingo games at the Memorial Centre in Kingston. She played ten cards at a time, and this is when they had little red buttons to put on the cards. Her friend came late and didn't get a card for the big jackpot that night, so my grandmother bought several and gave her one. Yes, she yelled *bingo* with one of my grandmother's cards and won two thousand dollars.

I was so excited I couldn't wait to tell my dad when we got home. The first thing he asked was how much of the prize money she gave to my grandmother, since it was her card. Thinking like my mother, my grandmother said, "Nothing, and I didn't expect anything." Well, did those two ever get into it. I don't know what made Dad angrier, the fact she didn't get any of the money or that she kept saying she didn't expect anything from her. I can hear the hollering to this day, and still believe I caused the fight. That's why I never give lottery tickets as gifts: it leads to hard feelings for me if they are winners. I believe this type of thinking is genetic, wired in your brain. No amount of explanation or rationalization can sway this logic and life is tougher for it, and you probably do get old before your time.

Mom once told me that she was so naive when it came to hockey that she actually thought Dad would play out his whole career in Hershey. Little did she know that, after he played in Hershey for one more year, her world would implode. Dad got traded, and not to just any team, but to the Springfield Indians, and it's there that he met Eddie Shore, the Darth Vader of hockey, for the first time. It was a simple fix, she thought: just tell the team you can't go. Dad had to explain to her that that wasn't how it worked—if she wanted to eat and have clothes on her back he had to go where they sent him. This is a woman who lived with her parents up until she married and had never been outside of Hershey. I asked her what this feeling was like. All she told me was that her mother said, "You're married now, and your life is with your husband." She was to move to a new city with a baby in tow and live in a rented semi-furnished apartment, taking only what would fit into a car. I couldn't imagine it. Talk about testing your love.

You can imagine what a tearful goodbye that meant for her family. They had to decide where to live between hockey seasons. The decision was made to move back and live with Dad's parents in Kingston. This made sense, for Dad was always guaranteed a summer job with the Public Utilities Commission there. All that my grandmother said to her daughter was, "Tootsie, when you hit that border be sure to put on your sweater." She did this so much that my paternal great-grandmother even mentioned it, always asking if Rosemarie was sick because she always had her sweater on. My mother always said she got along famously with Dad's parents, Maudie and Del. It was his mother who kept him in check when it came to being a married man. For instance, if he went out with the boys drinking after work one too many times in a week, it was Maudie—Anna, to the family—who mentioned he was now a married man with a child, and to smarten up. My mother probably didn't care, but to my grandmother this was unacceptable. I called my grandmother "Anna" one time. I heard her say she hated it when grandchildren called their grandparents "Nanna." I was so young yet such a brat that I tried calling her that, but it came out "Anna," so it stuck. As a youngster, my grandpa gave Dad heck for not coming home after work on a Friday to cut the grass. So even when he was married and a father, he had to toe the line with his own parents.

This arrangement went on for years. It meant that after every hockey season, whether in Springfield, Spokane, Three Rivers, Sudbury, Kitchener or wherever, we left after the season was over. This made Mom and me very adaptable. My main memories as a young kid are driving in the backseat with about two feet of area to play in. Dad would have a rod strapped across the backseat to hook clothes to. I always remember the clicking noise while driving at night. Looking back, I figured out it was the high beams that Dad would be flicking on and off, the switch located on the floor. I was never to ask if we were there yet, or say that I had to go to the bathroom. We had routine stops, and I had better go then or else. If I got restless, Dad would always ask me to look out for bears.

After a couple of years of this, my Uncle Rich, his wife Lillian, and his son Steven were in the same predicament. Uncle Rich also played professional hockey and needed somewhere to live in the summers. This was one tiny house at 518 Albert Street in Kingston, which at that point had eight people living in it, including two kids under three. To say this was a high-stress situation would be an understatement. Aunt Lillian wasn't as adaptable as my mom, and it didn't help that my dad teased her to no end. She used to smoke in the bathroom upstairs, and my dad would say he smelled smoke and ask if there was a fire somewhere. He was always making her cry, and it didn't help that my mom and uncle got along tremendously. It got to a point where my grandmother had to tell Dad to knock it off.

One summer, Dad and Uncle Rich decided to rent a house in Westport, Ontario, to try it as a living arrangement. The only thing I remember about this was a fight about Dad's dog, Dudgeon. My grandmother was before her time, for she would get all her dogs spayed or neutered. My grandfather used to say he'd better watch it or she'd have him fixed too. I didn't know at the time what all this meant, but everyone laughed and agreed. Dad insisted that Dudgeon was moving out with them. Anna argued and said the dog would not be happy, and she was correct. The dog kept running away and they had to tie him up, which he wasn't used to, and at night he would pant out of nerves. The whole house said the dog had to go back. There was a big argument, with my dad yelling, "If my dog isn't welcome here, neither am I!" and he left with the dog. As a child I was horrified, but my mother didn't seem too worried. Sure enough he returned after a few days, for his mother said, "Fine, the dog can stay, but you can't," so he came back home.

Wherever we lived in the winter, I always looked forward to returning to Kingston. It is good for kids to move around a lot. I hear parents today who do not want to uproot their children, and I can never figure that out. I made friends no matter where I lived, even if it was only for a hockey season. When I left it was no big deal, been nice knowing you, toodaloo.

I carried this into my adult life. I've been to many going-away parties for staff members where everyone is sad, crying and hugging, and I just don't get it. When Dad got the coaching job in Boston I had to change high schools in my senior year—no big deal. As a little girl, I loved moving back to Kingston and spending time with my grandmother. She raised me during the summer. I don't have one memory of my mother in those summers at Kingston. I guess she needed a break from me, and was more than willing to give my grandmother all the parental chores.

But my grandmother was tough on me. Manners, manners, manners—how she harped on, and she was concerned about my weight, even at that young age (too much chips and dip with babysitters). She would make me go to my great-grandmother's house for a visit, which I hated. I once told her I didn't want to go because there was nothing to do, her food and candy were stale, her drinks were warm, and it smelled old. Boy, did she yell at me to smarten up, and rightly so. I sure was a brat.

Then she started to take me to her part-time job, which I absolutely loved. She worked as an evening receptionist at Robert J. Reid & Sons Funeral Home. I learned many life lessons there, plus how to play gin rummy and shuffle cards. I was so proud that I had learned to back-shuffle cards, which made noise. She told me not to do it because people would hear. Looking back, I can see that's amusing.

Her job was to greet the people as they came to the viewings. There were always two to three bodies there at night, and she knew everyone who came through the door. She was so charming, knowing what and how to say things, and I learned a lot listening to her. But as lovely as she seemed, boy, was she tough on people. Hearing the wailing of people in a viewing room, I once said, "Boy, sounds like she really loved that person." Her demeanour changed and she said, "Don't let that crying impress you. In a couple of minutes they will be downstairs, laughing away." Sure enough they were, and she brought me to the top of the stairs to listen while saying, "Never be impressed with stuff like that. It's all a show for other people." Boy, did that lesson sink in. I think of her when I hear people say in the most insincere way at the end of telephone calls, "Love you." That "love you" is for the people listening, not the person on the other end of the phone.

At the end of the night my job was to turn off the lights in all the rooms. One night I asked her if I could look at the bodies up close in the caskets. She said, "Of course you can. It's not the dead people that will hurt you, it's the live ones." I couldn't get over all the beautiful jewellery they had on when I gazed into the coffins. I returned and said to her, "Boy, they must be really rich to bury all those rings and pretty necklaces." Again she said, "Don't be impressed with that, Cindy, it's all for show. When they are closing that casket, they will be pulling those rings off their fingers." Yikes.

People would always approach her and ask her to change something before the viewing started, like the person's hair, or they would say they "never smiled like that." She'd go up to the body and do whatever was needed. I marvelled at this. People used to ask my mother how she could let me spend so much time at a funeral parlour. Her response was simple: "She wants to." My mother and I knew everything had to be perfect when Anna died. Just before the viewing, much to our horror, we realized she didn't have any earrings on. My grandmother never left the house without earrings. Without hesitation, my mother took off her favourite earrings and clipped them on my grandmother's ears. Now that is love, and not the boo-hoo type.

I was the apple of my paternal grandfather's eye. He always said he'd wanted a girl, and now he had one. He was a huge, strapping man who made an impression on people due to his stature. Even at three years old I can remember him being a mysterious man that you would be in awe of, yet so kind and gentle to me. He was always smoking with a long black cigarette holder, looking regal. He would ask me to go and get his red package of Du Mauriers and matches. His ashtray had a bean-bag bottom with glass on top, and it had a ceramic Bulldog head on it. It's funny what you remember as a kid. One of my favourite things was walking to the store with him to buy cigarettes, and he would let me pick out any candy of my choice. All he said about smoking to me was that it was fine for him to do it, but not me. I never asked why not, but I heeded his warning. I guess all smokers to some degree know that it can't be good for you, but when you're on nicotine, you're addicted. He succumbed to brain cancer in the summer of 1962. My Mom's father, Noonoo, and his nephew Little Johnny drove up from Hershey to Kingston for the funeral. Noonoo died in a car accident on the way home, a family tragedy for all.

CHAPTER 10
MINOR HEADACHES (1962–1963)

*T*he dynamics of the family all changed after Mom lost her father in that accident. The decision was made to start staying in Hershey for the off-season, not Kingston. My maternal grandmother was not doing well with the unexpected death of her husband. I had never spent a whole summer living there, so once again this would be a new experience for the five-year-old me.

Life was a lot different there in many ways. First of all, Dad had to find a summer job. In Kingston he routinely had a job waiting for him at the Public Utilities Commission. His only skill after hockey was in construction. Luckily for him, the Hershey Corporation had just purchased the rights to make my favourite chocolate treat, Reese's Peanut Butter Cups, from H. B. Reese. This meant they were to build a new factory in Hershey, which was good news for our family. I never eat a peanut butter cup that doesn't make me think of Dad sweating it out, building the place where they are made.

To understand how tough it is to work construction in Hershey, you must know their weather. It is a small town nestled in a small valley. It gets extremely hot there, but worse yet is the humidity. They used to have a clock downtown on Chocolate Avenue that gave you the time, temperature, and humidity. It would often read 100°F and 100 percent humidity, and it wouldn't be raining. I'd like to mention that this street is lined with Hershey Kisses streetlights. Two of these lights stood in front of the arena where Dad's Major Junior A Mississauga IceDogs played, because the rink was originally called the Hershey Centre. Mississauga was also gracious enough to make its address 5500 Rose Cherry Place. This building now goes by another name and those unique lights are long gone. I often wondered what happened to them. Hershey Canada also stepped up to the plate when we were looking for a founding patron to give $100,000 towards the campaign to build Rose Cherry's Home for Kids. As you can see, the city of Hershey has many meanings to the Cherry family, including being where my brother and I were born.

Dad would come home from a long day of working in the sun and collapse from exhaustion. My job was to take off his construction boots before he went into the house. We had a huge cement porch with a roof off to the side. Sometimes he would fall asleep right there, since the inside would be even hotter with no A/C. When I think of the players today and how they train off-season, it makes me laugh. They live a sweet life, and the thought of them having to work in the summer is unheard of. I don't think Dad ever lifted a weight in his life when he played. The extent of his workouts would be to go for a run. This would not be the same as the joggers today. He would run full tilt as fast as he could, slow down, and run fast again. The shape he went to training camp in was usually better than when he left. This is hard to believe, for oh, how my mom's family could cook. They were typical Italians in the fact they had a functional kitchen in the basement and a beautiful fancy kitchen on the main floor, where you were only allowed to eat cereal or toast. The food was unbelievable, and it was here that I started my downward spiral into fatness. I loved their food!

Just like in Kingston, my life in Hershey was fun and filled with friends. It was there I learned to ride a bicycle. I remember my dad telling me I had to get rid of my training wheels. I resisted, so he took them off and threw them in the garbage. He took me to a gravel alley behind the house, and there I learned fast. If I didn't want scraped knees I had better find my balance fast, so I did. How did I ever survive with no helmet?

There were lots of fireflies and butterflies to catch. Speaking of butterflies reminds me of one of the many combative conversations between Dad and Ron. They spent hours together travelling for HNiC, which included shopping. Ron saw a beautiful butterfly display he wanted to buy for his father. Dad questioned the saleswoman, "How could anyone be a butterfly admirer when you know what they do to these beautiful creatures?" Having a pin put through your body is not exactly a favourable thing to do if you admire their beauty. Of course, once Ron heard Dad question this (with a hint of disgust), you know he had to have it, if for no other reason than to "bug" Dad (that sounds like a Ron pun). I, like Dad, think those framed butterfly displays are macabre.

Most of my memorable fun things happened at Hershey Park, which the founder, Milton Hershey, built for his employees and the local community. It was on acres and acres of land and featured four different pools, all separated by beautiful white sand. There was a circular kiddie pool, an adults-only pool, an anything-goes pool, and a diving-only section. There was a rickety wooden bridge you'd walk to the canteen on. Under this bridge was a shallow stream filled with colourful carp. It was fun to throw food over so they would all come together, and you'd see all that flashing gold as they ate.

I remember one eventful day when my dad took me solo to the pool. I was too old to go into the men's locker room with Dad, so I had to go through the ladies' part. Somehow I lost my key and the man at the door would not let me leave without returning it. I knew my dad was waiting for me and I started to get upset. I then heard Dad yelling for me and I peeked out. He asked me what was going on and, about to burst into tears, I explained that this man wouldn't let me through unless I found my key. I remember the look Dad gave the guy, but he stood his ground. He said something about how I'd have to pay for it if I lost my key. I could see there would be big trouble, so I just ran out. I remember thinking I was more afraid for the guy and what Dad would do to him than being scared about the key or him being angry with me for losing it. I think that says something about my perception of my dad. Eventually we stopped going to this park and I couldn't figure out why. I mistakenly asked my grandma, and all she said was, "'Cause the Harrisburg people go." I didn't know what that meant; all I knew was I never felt the same way about Pennsylvania's capital.

Life in Hershey was a challenge for Dad. My mom had many relatives there who were a lot different than what Dad was used to. The biggest adjustment was how they raised their kids. They were undisciplined, and to say they were loud and obnoxious is an understatement. When you're a kid, you tend to take on the persona of your friends. They had tons of toys, which I did not, and they had no respect for them. But they liked playing with mine and always broke them, and I'd cry relentlessly about it. I will never forget I had a toy plane made of metal that made sound effects when its rubber wheels came down, and it lit up. It had travelled many miles with me and kept me occupied for hours in the back seat when we were driving to who knows where. When some second cousins got ahold of my plane, it took about three minutes until one wing was torn off and the landing legs were broken. I cried and cried. It was the first time my dad got angry with Mom about her relatives.

As kids, we all have memorable moments of discipline. One of my most dramatic (or should that be *traumatic*) experiences came at about five years old while watching a horse show at the open coliseum at Hershey Park. It was, as usual, a sweltering day. This coliseum had bench seating. All my so-called semi-cousins were there. I don't know how they were all related to me; I never could figure out who was who, for there were so many of them. They were running around the seats, bothering all the other spectators. Dad told me several times to sit down, but the call to run around with the pack was just too great for me to resist. All of a sudden my dad grabbed me and said that was it. He and I proceeded to the car while I kicked and screamed. I did want to be there, and I'd be good, I told him. My mom did not follow, and she was peeved. Dad and I sat in the boiling black car with a black interior for what seemed like hours. I cried the whole time, wondering when Mom would return. I remember seeing the drips of sweat running off my dad's nose. Finally we saw the masses returning to their vehicles, which meant the show was over, and even then Mom took her time getting to the car. It was a silent ride home. I stopped crying out of fear of a big fight. Needless to say, when he told me to sit down in the future, I listened. It was a lesson I will never forget.

When Del was four, he received a similar life lesson. To this day, if he ever hears anyone answer with "good" when asked how they are doing, he will look at me and shake his head. I learned from my dad that sometimes one of these memorable moments will linger for years. It's like you are teaching your kid that you are nuttier than they are, and I proved it to Del.

It was the first home game of the Mississauga IceDogs after Christmas that year. I warned my son that, since everyone knew him, they were going to ask him how his Christmas was. Under no circumstances did I want him to say the dreaded "good," which the rest of the kids would grunt when asked the question. He was to say, "Fine, thank you." I told him they would then ask him what he got for Christmas, and he was to have an answer right away. In this case, it was a Buzz Lightyear toy. I reminded him on the drive there and we practiced what he was to say. I told him that if he didn't say "fine, thank you," we would go directly home and there would be no hockey game for him. Some people might think this is extreme, but I, like my dad, believe that not being portrayed as a spoiled brat is very important, and manners are everything. We walked in through the main gate of the Hershey Centre and the first person we ran into was the food and beverage manager, Janet Jones, and she asked the fateful question. Del's response: "Good." Trust me, he was not saying it to test whether I would follow through with the punishment. I think he realized his fatal mistake immediately and started yelling, "I'm sorry!" I grabbed him and he went limp. I dragged him through the slushy snow back to the car as he cried and yelled, "I'm sorry, Mommy! I'll start saying 'fine, thank you'!" It was a scene—everyone was looking, and some knew who we were because I could hear the whispers: "That's the Cherry family"— isn't that nice? We stayed in the car for about thirty minutes. He asked me innocently, in between his hyperventilating and crying, why people care if he had a nice Christmas. I admit my answer was way above a four-year-old's comprehension. I told him it's what people do to make conversation. I even tried to explain that his manners were an indication of whether I was a good parent. I am sure that went way over his head too, but I tried to explain this philosophy when he was older, and his response was, "As usual, it's all about you." I responded unequivocally, "Without a doubt." I truly believe an unruly, spoiled brat is reflective of the parents. I hold this same philosophy with dogs. Ask anyone who deals with dogs, a vet tech, kennel worker, or, better yet, a dog groomer like me. Kooky dog and kooky kids usually means lenient parents, equating discipline with meanness.

In case you're wondering, we did go back into the game. He must have been asked ten times about his Christmas and what Santa brought him, and his reply was right on the money. To this day you will never hear Don Cherry's grandson utter the word "good." If you do, think of him as too old to rebel against his mother, because that is what he will be doing. As he would say, it's all about me.

In 1963 Dad was traded to Rochester from the Spokane Comets, which was good timing. I was ready for kindergarten, my brother Tim was born, and it was time to put down roots. When asked where I was raised, I will always answer Rochester. Grade school, junior high, and high school are the most impressionable years. For my parents, it felt that all of Dad's life lessons would be applied there, too. The transitions were from player to unemployment, back to being a player, then coaching, with the ultimate goal being reached: to make it to the NHL. It all happened when we moved to Rochester. That's where I think we all grew up, and the Cherry family will always have a soft spot in our hearts for Flower City.

CHAPTER 11

SETTING DOWN ROOTS IN FLOWER CITY (1963–1966)

The move from Spokane, Washington, back east to Rochester, New York, was a welcomed one. I was starting kindergarten, so what better time to set down roots? Mom and Dad rented a house, which was huge to me then, as opposed to the apartments we had previously rented in our travels. I googled 217 Mohawk Street to see what it looks like now and, as usual, my childhood memories were out of proportion.

I walked to school in the morning, went home for lunch, and then walked home. This was fine till winter came. I was one house shy of being able to stay at school for lunch. In those days you did not measure snowfall by inches or centimetres, but by the foot. When Dad came home early from practice one day and saw me plodding through three feet of snow, he'd had enough. He called the school, made a ruckus, and presto, I could bring my lunch to school. *Oh*, I thought, *that's the power of my dad.*

That house was a fixer-upper, and though it was a rental Dad did his share of renovations. He was handy and prided himself on being a great house painter. Little did he know that he'd be doing it for a living after he retired from hockey. He claimed that this skill came from having a summer job when he was young in Kingston with an old-timer named Mr. Cornwall. He was well known in the city and painted many of the older estate homes, so he had to do it correctly the first time. Mr. Cornwall paid him well, but unfortunately taught him bad work ethics, or so his father thought.

One afternoon his father came home for lunch and Dad was still sleeping. When he asked Grandma Anna why Donald was still in bed, she said, "Mr. Cornwall thought it might rain today." Well, that was all he had to hear. When Dad got up, he was told to give Mr. Cornwall his notice and find a new job. He got him a job working on a section gang, a tough job building and maintaining railroad tracks. It's what you often see prisoner chain gangs working on in the movies as punishment. To work in the blazing sun with creosote-treated railroad ties and men who were hardened and tough was an incredible wakeup call for a seventeen-year-old kid. These hardened guys picked on him unmercifully. They'd ride him about only getting the job because of his dad, and that he wasn't tough enough to do a man's job.

One day he couldn't take it anymore and grabbed the ringleader of his torment. He put a pickaxe to this guy's head and said, "One more word and I'm putting this right through your head." The guy didn't say a word and Dad let him go. From then on he was one of the guys. Dad often claims this job gave him hair on his chest. However, it did not last long either.

One day his mother was in the car with his Uncle Bill, who was married to Grandpa's sister Hilda. I remember him as a slight man who was quiet and charming and always smoked a pipe that smelled oh-so good. When they drove by a section gang, he pointed out to her that was what Donald was doing now. My grandmother was aghast and couldn't believe it, so Dad got notice to quit that job, too. He really didn't care, because the Junior A hockey season was just about to start and he was now in great shape and ready for camp.

Getting back to the house on Mohawk Street, the fixer-upper, I would occasionally go up to the scary attic. The last owner, I guessed, bred parakeets and let them fly free up there. It was nice for the birds, but what a mess. Mom had to scrape all the bird feces from the walls. I don't think Mom and Dad knew how much work needed to be done to this house till they moved in. The walls had significant cracks in the plaster all over the place. It was especially bad by the staircase leading to the second floor. Rather than taping and re-drywalling them, which would have been expensive, Dad had his own way of doing things. He stuccoed everything, and even Mom had fun doing it. Dad bugged her about leaving the pointy bumps too high. They were awful deadly, and if you scraped by them going down the staircase you'd end up bleeding. Once he was telling her how she was doing it wrong, pinching her and eating a ham sandwich. Well, he had bugged her one too many times, and she swiped him with a full brush of plaster right in his mouth. He coughed and spat plaster and ham all over the place. All she said was, "Look at the mess you made! Now I'll have to clean that up." The little Italian girl from Hershey was toughening up. Perhaps she got her panache from her mother-in-law.

Once my grandmother told my mom a story after Dad complained about her serving him too many spaghetti dinners. You have to wonder what he expected after marrying an Italian. My grandfather would call home every day at noon to ask what they were having for dinner. One day she asked him what he would like for dinner, and he said he wanted creamed onions. He came home in a bad mood, got ready for dinner, sat down, and started going on and on about how he didn't like the creamed onions she had cooked. She got up and, in front of my dad and uncle, poured the pot of onions over his head. Dad said he remembered the incident vividly and almost peed his pants, fearing what might come next. When I asked what the outcome was, he said she just walked out of the house and didn't come home till the next day in defiance. Grandpa just wiped the onions away and ate the rest of the dinner doused in creamed onions in silence. She was no pushover when it came to keeping her husband in line.

She once told me about Grandpa having guys over to play poker. They ate, drank, and played late into the night, and all the while he was yelling for more food and booze. She finally ran out of food to feed them. When they kept yelling for sandwiches in the wee hours of the night, she opened several cans of dog food and added relish, lots of salt and pepper, and mayonnaise for a delicious spread on bread, and they thought these late-night sandwiches were delicious.

I know Mom enjoyed setting down roots. She knew Dad had found his place in hockey as a player with the Rochester Americans— the "Amerks," as they were known. I always smirked a bit when people would write or comment about him and make a point of mentioning he had only played one game in the NHL. To emphasize this point when describing his career indicates that they don't know much about hockey, or are just trying to prove some point.

When you look at the roster of the Amerks in the sixties, you see that you had many past and future NHLers: Jim Pappin, Al Arbour, Bronco Horvath, Stan Smrke, Gerry Ehman, Ed Litzenberger, Gerry Cheevers, Larry Hillman, Jim McKenny . . . the list is endless. Whether they were on their way to the big time or just winding down their careers, Mom and Dad saw them all. They also saw some players start with them, make it, and then humble their way back to where they started. Dad often tells stories about when players made it to the NHL and walked by him without acknowledging his existence when they had training camps together.

I think these players might be a little bitter at winding down their careers with the Amerks, and who could blame them. Take a player like Eddie Litzenberger. Here's a guy who played with the Canadiens, Blackhawks, Red Wings, and Maple Leafs, who found himself playing with a confirmed minor-leaguer (Dad's quote, not mine) like Don Cherry. Dad had no bitterness or jealousy toward these players, but he'd let them know when they got out of line. Such was the case with Mr. Litzenberger. They were having a team meal one afternoon, and for some reason Eddie started bugging his own starting goalie, Gerry Cheevers. He kept saying, "I'm going to hurt you tonight. It might even be in the warm-up." He could see this was rattling Gerry and kept it up. Finally Dad chimed in, "Eddie, I'm going to the washroom, and if I hear you say that one more time when I get back, you're going to get it." Sure enough he kept it up, so Dad took a butter knife (he told me that it was not a steak knife, which in Dad's eyes made a difference), grabbed Eddie around the neck, put the knife to his throat, and said, "Say it again." Eddie stopped.

I know this story because I was once sat at a table at a fundraising event in Niagara Falls where Dad was a speaker with Mr. Litzenberger. I knew he had played with Dad in Rochester, and I was trying to have a conversation with him about those times. I was getting the brush off, so I got the message loud and clear. I told Dad how grumpy I thought he was, and he told me why he wasn't the biggest fan of Don Cherry. That explained it all, and I had to laugh.

It was always amusing when Dad and I went out to celebrity events. He'd encounter many retired NHLers who had snubbed him in one way or another. Remember, most of the training camps were combined with the farm teams. I could always feel the coolness from Dad when we came into the company of one of these guys. One time he was a step away from being rude to one such player, which wasn't his usual way. On the ride home, I mentioned to him about how he was a bit cool to this guy, and he let me have it. He went on a spiel about how in 1961 he wouldn't give Dad the time of day, and he wasn't about to acknowledge his existence now. Still, it must have been hard for those guys to see this confirmed fifth defenseman minor-leaguer be the toast of the town some fifty years later. You could sometimes see this on Coach's Corner: if Ron asked Dad about some old-timer, like Red Kelly, he would shrug and let poor Ron hang there with silent airtime. I'd know there was a good story there, for Dad is like an elephant—he never forgot those guys.

My mother also witnessed these circumstances of players rising to the top and then descending into the minors. Can you imagine how she felt? In Dad's day, in the sixties, his top salary may have been around $4200. As a child you never think about money until something makes you ponder. The richest person I ever encountered when I was young was the Amerk's team doctor, Mr. Lordy. After each game, the wives and children would wait outside the dressing room. Mrs. Lordy and her brood would also mingle with the players' wives. Though the wives dressed nicely, it was nothing compared to what a doctor's wife could afford. She always had furs on. In those days, wearing fur was the ultimate statement that you had made it.

Years later, this was evident when Mom and I went into the Bruins' wives' room. It was like a dead Noah's Ark hanging on the coat rack. Though you don't know it at that time, it is at this young age that impressions are made that you carry for years to come. Not only did the doctor's wife look stunning, but her kids were equally as showy in telling us about all the great toys they had. They'd constantly brag about their stuff, and Christmas was a nightmare listening to them. I am sure it never bothered the other kids, but being a Cherry and a chip off the old block, it bugged me.

At the end of the War Memorial Rink where we waited, there was a massive stage with tall, thick velvet curtains. They were so much fun to play in and we'd play hide and seek throughout this area. Being the ringleader, and resenting the Lordy kids, I would not let them engage in our fun. They'd go crying to their mommy, saying we were mean to them, which I guess we were. Perhaps in this day and age they may call this bullying, I don't know. Mom always used to say to me on the ride home that she didn't understand why I wouldn't play nice with those kids. I told her they bragged too much about their toys. Dad laughed, for he didn't like them either. I guess they'd come into the dressing room, not knowing their place, and get away with it because of who they were. So it was music to Dad's ears that I didn't like them. When I saw that Dad laughed, I perked up and said, "See, Dad doesn't like them either." Boy, did Mom get angry. She started yelling at me, saying that from then on I had to let them play. At the next game when all the kids began to play, I sat in the seats by the ice. All the kids asked me to join them, and I said I wasn't playing anymore. I suppose this was cutting off my nose to spite my face, which, unfortunately, still applies today, and it is not a good trait to have. But trust me, not many of the other kids played once the Lordy kids got into the fray, so I made my point.

This trait of not liking braggers must be hereditary. Fast-forward about thirty-eight years later, to when I'm a parent. There were not many kids in our neighbourhood to play with, so I tried to talk my son into playing with one of the kids up the street who was about the same age. He refused adamantly, which made me angry, and I asked the kid to come over anyway. Before he arrived I asked Del why he didn't like him, and he told me he bragged too much. I eavesdropped on their conversation as they played baseball in the empty lot beside my house, and what Del said was true: he talked about how good he was at golf and baseball, going on and on. It was the last time I asked the kid over. I think back on what I preached to Del in his younger years; I didn't figure much was sinking in, but I guess I was mistaken. I told him that no one likes a bragger, and he should never play "I can top that," even though he probably could, but that's not how to make friends.

He applied that philosophy once when I picked him and his buddies up from a golf camp. I asked, "How'd you do today?" and all I got was, "OK." His friends piped up and told me he had shot an eagle, and two birdies in the nine holes they played. I tried to backtrack from my earlier teachings and told him it's not bragging if it's true. To see if this had sunk in, I asked my brother to ask Del how his golf game went that day. Once again, all he said was, "OK."

I saw this happen again in a more pronounced way. Del played Tyke hockey with Max Domi. Max's mom Leanne and I were good friends, with the same philosophies on raising our children: we were tough on them. We were the opposite of many of our peers, to say the least. In other words, we were no granola or helicopter moms and didn't worry about peanuts, if you get my drift.

One Sunday morning I drove Max and Del to their Tyke practice. If you can believe it, three or four of the other players had been at the Leafs game the night before, Del and Max included. These kids did nothing but brag in the dressing room about going to the game and getting autographs during the warm-up because their seats were along the ice. They went on and on, making the other players envious of how lucky they were, and their fathers were just as bad. But Del and Max sat in silence, not saying a word. Max's dad Tie was playing and Del's grandfather was on Coach's Corner, and neither of them said a word. I was so proud of them. When I dropped Max off, I told Leanne what had transpired and said that we were definitely on the right path in raising these socially acceptable kids. This should be the goal of all parents, not to be their kids' friends.

To say Leanne and I are not alarmist mothers is an understatement. We are such good friends because of our mutual hockey background. I was born into the hockey world and lived through my dad being a player, coach, and hockey broadcaster. Leanne married an NHLer and gave birth to one. We covered all the bases within the hockey world. We have a lot of great stories to tell, but there are only a few I will share.

She may not like me telling this story, but it is amusing. At five years old, Del came home complaining that he had fallen at recess and hurt his arm. There were no scrapes or blood and I felt it was only tender in one spot. He could move readily, so I thought it was only bruised. I told him he had hockey practice that night and a game the next, and since he played goal just to shrug it off. He was still whining about it two days later, so I figured I would take him to emergency to get it checked out. I say to the triage nurse, "I hope it's not broken, because he has played hockey several times this past week." She rolled her eyes at me and said they had to X-ray it, and to wait in the lobby. Sure enough, the doctor came out and said, "Will the mother that let her child play hockey with a broken arm please come this way." I went with it, raising my arm and saying, "Yeah, that would be me." All eyes looked my way.

They put a cast on it and he could hardly wait to tell his grandpa, who immediately autographed it, writing, "Them's the breaks." Dad thought this was so great that he mentioned on his radio show with Brian Williams how tough his grandson was because he played goal with a broken arm. I am sure all the listeners asked themselves, *What kind of mother does that kid have?* I told Leanne how awful I felt about letting my son play sports with a broken limb. Weeks later she called me up and asked me, "Remember that exclusive club you started for moms that let their children play sports with broken bones? Well, add me as a member."

Max played soccer, lacrosse, and hockey in the summers, and had started complaining about a sore leg. In tough-mom style, Leanne said, "Suck it up. Hockey players play hurt." After a week or so it was still bugging him, so Tie took him to the Leafs' doctor for an X-ray. Sure enough, it was broken. He went to school in a full-leg cast. Granola mothers might be cringing reading this, but alas, they wouldn't read this type of book anyway, so I am safe.

Del and Max were into hockey. Why wouldn't they be? They had good hockey genes in them. However, I said to Leanne that I thought we should expand their horizons. She agreed and we got tickets to see *The Lion King* at a local theatre. However, it was on a Saturday night and the kids didn't want to go, but we said we'd take them to Gretzky's restaurant before the play. We figured we'd allow them a little hockey influence that night and told them to play dome hockey while we were having our coffee. As they were playing, a TV crew walked in, went up to Del and Max, and put them on camera, saying, "This looks like two little hockey players. Are you guys going to the Leafs game tonight?" They looked sad and said, "No, our moms are making us see the Lion King tonight." Leanne and I were killing ourselves laughing—if that crew only knew whom they were talking to.

They also went to nursery school together. Once, when they were only about three or four years old, I was picking Del up from school and he jumped in the car angrily, saying, "I will never play with Max again." I asked why, and he told me that they were picking soccer teams and Max came up with names for them: his team became the Toronto Super Stars and Del's was dubbed the Mississauga Dirty Diapers. It was all I could do to not kill myself from laughing. Not one to coddle or console my son's sadness, I said, "If you are stupid enough to let Max name your team, then you should be called that."

I loved watching Max play—you could see he was a Domi just by how he skated. I noted to Leanne one day, "Look how he drags one skate behind him when he is coming to a stop . . . his dad used to do that." I always enjoyed going to IceSports in Etobicoke on Friday nights to watch the Minor Midget Triple-A games and see him play with other future NHLers. It was a who's who of hockey, with CHL scouts, famous hockey Dads (Gilmour, Clark, Thomas) and the odd celebrity, like dad scouting with my brother or Bobby Orr putting on his agent hat. It didn't hurt that they had a great bar, so you could watch all four rinks while having a pop or two.

So, life was good in Rochester, and for a professional athlete's family that meant winning. Rochester won the Calder Cup in 1964-65 and 1965-66, went to the finals in 1966-67, and won again in 1967-68. This means Dad was getting playoff money and it was time to move again. This time it was for all the right reasons, as Mom and Dad bought their first house in 1966.

CHAPTER 12

MOVIN' ON UP

Mom and Dad were moving on up, as *The Jeffersons'* theme song describes. The first house they bought was an English-style Tudor at 181 Elm Drive. I started fourth grade at the stately-looking Charles Carrol Public School #46. It was the closest you could be to the suburbs without leaving the city. I mention this because there is a slight difference between Elm Street and Elm Drive in Rochester.

Let me explain. You may remember CBC's television program series in 2004 to determine the top 10 greatest Canadians. Dad was voted #7, ahead of Sir John A. MacDonald, Alexander Graham Bell, and Wayne Gretzky, much to the chagrin of the CBC. The number one spot went to Tommy Douglas, the father of Medicare and the premier of Saskatchewan. Now, not to take away from Douglas's accomplishments, but there was a rumour from a reliable source about how Dad ended up in seventh spot. It was theorized that since there was no overall limit on the number of times one could cast a vote in the final polling, the teachers of Canada saw it as their civic duty to get Mr. Douglas in there. They had students voting to ensure that a person like Don Cherry didn't reach the first spot. Our family was surprised and grateful that he made it into the top 10. When asked about it Dad tried to be as humble as he could, distinguishing between the greatest and the most popular, which is why he thought he was nominated.

Each nominee got an advocate to host a one-hour show on CBC to say why their candidate should be in the top 10. With Ron hosting the show, Bret Hart, the five-time World Wrestling Federation title holder, was to be Dad's advocate. The producer called me for inside information. I had no idea what it was for, because no one knew who the top 10 were at that time. I was reluctant to cooperate, for what if she was doing a hatchet job on Dad and I helped her out? After all, she did say she was working for the CBC. She finally swore me to secrecy and let me in on why she needed some information on Dad. To sweeten the pot, she told me how CBC was sabotaging her efforts to do a good job. There were ten shows being produced simultaneously, with limited editing time and budgeting. She told me they were giving her lousy editing time hours and not being very cooperative with her needs. It would be no surprise to me that CBC would not want Dad to be in the top 10, so she wouldn't be a priority. Hearing that, well, game on. I gave them a lot of unique and fun info, including where we lived in Rochester, because they wanted to visit the old house.

One day I got a panicky phone call from the producer in Rochester, saying she couldn't find the house. She sounded a bit nervous about the neighbourhood, despite having Bret Hart with her. It turns out they went to Elm Street, not Elm Drive, which is in the inner city of Rochester. In its day it was one of the city's toughest neighbourhoods, and from her voice it sounded like it still was. She was glad to be in the company of Bret Hart, and they got out of there fast. I then told her the next-door neighbour's name, Mrs. Bauman, in case she still lived there. She rang their doorbell to introduce herself and Bret and the mission they were on, and sure enough she still lived there. She invited them in for coffee and they had a friendly chat about the Cherrys. I know I'm biased, but the show's producer did a great job of making it interesting and enjoyable. The other shows were dry and factual but not very entertaining. Despite being out of his element, Bret did an excellent job of making it more natural for him to believe in his candidate. When they showed the old house, I became a bit melancholy. I wish I could watch that show again, but no matter what I search for it's nowhere to be found. What a shame.

The house on Elm Drive was a fixer-upper once again. The first day we moved in, Dad started to peel off the wallpaper and found what looked like BB-gun pellet holes throughout the whole first floor. It was the first time I remember Mom crying over where we lived, with Dad saying, "Don't worry, Rose, I'll have it all dynamite-looking in no time." She just shook her head, but in the long run he kept his promise.

Seeing they had only lived in rentals, they looked forward to decorating to reflect their unique taste. It became even more extraordinary when Christine, the girlfriend of Jim McKenny, an up-and-coming star with the Toronto Maple Leafs, would come to visit him when he played in Rochester in 1968. Times were different then, and when a girlfriend came to visit they did not stay with the player, so she stayed with us. She had a flair for interior design, which she pursued as a career. The only bathroom in the house ended up with black-and-white polka-dot wallpaper, the black dots being velvet, with red-shag carpeting. The shower curtain had dots too. It was wild.

Jim McKenny was quite the character and hockey player in his time. He played on nine different teams in five other leagues during his career. In his NHL rookie year of 1969-70, he was second only to Bobby Orr in goals for a defenseman. He also coached and played on teams in France and Switzerland, and played for Team Canada in 1969. His longest stretch was with the Leafs: eight seasons. His off-ice life was as exciting as his hockey career. He had a leading role in a 1971 movie called *Face-Off*, was a high-fashion male model, and later became a sports broadcaster. He was a must on the banquet circuit due to his wit, charm, and good looks. He was a master of the one-liners, and his most famous was, "Half of the game is mental, and the other half is being mental," and he certainly owned up to that. Because this was more than just a joke, he was roomed with Dad on the road. I say "Jimmy," but he was also known as Howie, because of similar good looks and, let's say, *lifestyle* of Howie Young, known better as "Puck's Bad Boy."[16] Jimmy was handsome, charismatic, witty, and also tried his shot at acting after retirement, with roles in the TV mini-series *Lonesome Dove*, the 1997 TV film *Last Stand at Saber River* with Tom Selleck, and the movie *Young Guns 2*. No question, Jimmy was following the path of Howie Young in many ways.

When I look back on Dad and Jimmy's relationship, I cannot help but see the similarities to the movie *Bull Durham*. You could easily envision Dad being Kevin Costner's character, the seasoned minor-leaguer Crash Davis, with Jimmy as the Tim Robbins character, the up-and-coming superstar "Nuke" Laloosh. Management specifically roomed those two on the road together so Dad would look after Jim and try to curb his wild

---

[16] A play on writer George Wilbur Peck's fictional prankster "Peck's Bad Boy."

ways. He saw the talent in Jim that he himself never did, and could see how close he was to throwing it all away with his antics, just like Crash did with the Nuke. Dad was also Jim's protector from the other players taking advantage of this young rookie. He was a star, so he had more money than most players in the minors. This meant he paid for more than his share in bar tabs until Dad stepped in. Dad looked after the rookies, and he once told the story of how a player passed out some beer on a bus to every player plus the media guys on the trip but didn't give any to the rookies. Seeing the injustice in this, he stepped in and told the beer distributor that someday they would have to rely on those guys, and they were part of the team. They got their beer.

How much of Dad's guidance to Jim McKenny sunk in I do not know, but I do know they remained good friends far beyond their hockey careers. I sat with Mom, Dad, and Tim when Jimmy made his sportscaster debut on City-TV in Toronto. You could see his nervousness, which reminded me of the flop-sweat scene in the 1987 movie *Broadcast News*, where Albert Brooks, playing Aaron Altman, gets his one shot at being an on-air anchor. We were yelling at the TV, saying, "Come on, Jimmy, you can do it!" And he did. He was everyone's favourite on TV, with his wit and charm coming through every broadcast. Years later, we kept in touch when he had me groom his Bearded Collie in my mobile dog-grooming van. It was a pleasure catching up with him, even though he was not happy with me always having to shave his dog because of the matting. I'd say to him, as I did all my customers, "Either learn how to brush your dog or get it groomed on a regular schedule, or I'll just shave it." He was never amused.

This is a funny backstory that concerns *Bull Durham*. Fast-forward to 1999, when Dad was part owner of the OHL's Mississauga IceDogs. The buses had evolved since Dad's day, and they now showed movies. He told his new wife to go out and get some movies for the long road trips. Well, didn't she come back with *Bull Durham*, thinking it's a sports movie? Some of these kids were only sixteen years old, and if you remember, some of the talk and sex scenes in this movie are very vivid. Dad couldn't believe what he was watching on the bus and quickly turned it off.

Here is a scene right out of the movie *Slap Shot*. The houses on Elm Drive were very close together. The kitchen of the next house was right beside our side door from the driveway. Dad would come home during the summer from a hard day's work at Ridge Construction, a division of Kodak and their private construction company. When he came in through the side door there were three steps leading up to the kitchen and the staircase leading down to the basement. He'd take his muddy construction boots off on that landing and be greeted by his beloved dog Blue. He'd lie on the stairs, kissing and hugging her, telling her how beautiful and loved she was, and saying how much he loved her kisses. I don't know which she loved more, licking the sweat or the aftershave off Dad's face. The neighbour next door told Mom what a wonderful husband she had, hearing from her window the things that Don said to her when he got home from work. She only wished her husband was that affectionate. Did they ever get a laugh when Mom enlightened her that he was talking to the dog.

With the move to this new house, Dad's Amerks were doing quite well. Winning three Calder Cups meant playoff money, which meant significant luxuries, such as a sliding glass door leading to the back so Blue could easily access the fenced-in backyard. Plus, Mom and Dad splurged and bought an above-ground figure-eight pool. Simple pleasures for some, but for us it meant Dad was on a winning team.

It is here that I'd like to mention that examples like these, getting that sliding door or the pool itself, illustrate the importance hockey played in our lives. It may seem trivial now, but then such luxuries were dictated by the team's win/loss column. To most, hockey is a game for entertainment or something you play for fun and exercise. For the Cherry family, it was our life. Winning meant the playoffs, and, closer to the end, the championships. With this came happiness in many forms. Sure, there was the satisfaction of winning. This showed that all your family's sacrifices were well worth it. In many cases, such as whether the Bruins won against the Canadiens in the playoffs, the outcome determined if Dad would be back next year or fired. If he didn't return with the Bruins, it meant Mom and Dad would have to sell their beautiful house and move away to who knows where.

Sarah Manninen, who played my mother in the movie *Keep Your Head Up, Kid*, asked me about Mom's reaction to goals. Happiness, of course, but the glee never came through as much as the relief. No matter what team Dad coached, if they didn't win the consequences would affect the family. This was a fact, one that I accepted. In never questioning it, we were never resentful. Not all people have that attitude. One friend had a father who was a career hockey guy. Her young son was given the opportunity to go to a Leafs game, and she refused to let him go. I asked her why she would deny her son such fun, as he played minor hockey with Del. She expressed her anger and resentment toward the game, explaining that she resented the time it kept her father away from the family, and I started to laugh. He had never played pro, coached one season in the WHL, and was upper management on several Toronto teams, hardly the hardship that we as a family had experienced. I couldn't relate, for I saw hockey as a source of income and a livelihood for my father, not something I resented.

I asked a ten-year-old whose dad played pro if they were going to the game one night. She said, "No, I hate hockey." In front of her mother, I said, "You hate hockey, eh? Don't you know it's hockey that pays for your $900 custom-made riding boots? Or feeds your pampered horse? Do I need to go on? You better be damn thankful your dad plays hockey to keep you in all that expensive stuff you like so much." She just sneered and walked away, but her mother loved it.

I guess my point is this: it's all in the attitude that you want to believe in. Sure, I could have been much more resentful than my friend, but what's the point?

So, life in Rochester was great for the whole family. Mom and Dad had the house fixed up exactly how they wanted it, complete with a pool and slide. The off-seasons were as busy as the winters, when Dad and Mom ran their hockey school and Dad played in a bagpipe band. He played the tenor drum, the flashiest of the band's three different kinds. This was due to the combinations of different swings (a.k.a. flourishes) with the drumsticks they performed while marching. However, he did let me in on a secret about these drums: the sticks never hit them. It was all for show—go figure. The drumsticks had crocheted coverings with tassels at the rounded end to emphasize the routines. My grandmother knit them for the band. He practiced for hours in perfecting the routine of twirling these drumsticks into the air. They could have up to four drummers, and all had to be in sync for their complicated moves. He held on to them by the short, thin ropes that eventually cut into his fingers till they bled when he practiced. Mom would question why he wouldn't wear gloves, at least while he practiced. He said he lost "the feel." Sounds like Dad.

One time the bass drummer didn't show up for the parade and Dad volunteered to play it. This is a huge drum that you really have to pound on. Because of this, he decided to wear the white gloves. Dad finally being able to pound on a drum meant only one thing: hitting it *hard*. He had a big smile on his face in the parade, just wailing away as he marched by. I noticed how the paint was smearing all up on the drum where it said "Rochester Pipe Band," and, knowing Dad, he would not have been pleased about that. Turns out he was pounding so hard that he had made a hole in his gloves and worn down the skin on his fingers—it was his blood splattered all over the drum.

In Rochester, parades were popular in the seventies and very competitive. Every weekend Dad's band would participate in one. All the bands, whether military, bugle, drum corps, or pipe, would compete against each other within the counties of Rochester. Dad's band would constantly win, and had quite a lot of money in their coffers. This money paid for their uniforms and the booze at the picnics they had after every parade. The families made the food and each wife tried to outdo the others with their recipes. In the seventies, public parks in Rochester were not exactly the safest place to be; however, as we were with a bunch of kilt-wearing, drinking Scotchmen, we didn't have too much to worry about.

While marching they were a sight to behold, with their red tunics, thick white crossbelts, and waistbelt, and Dad wore a plaid brooch with a Cairngorm stone that his paternal grandmother had given him. Plus they wore ostrich-feathered bonnets, horsehair sporrans, knives called *sgian-dubhs* tucked into their argyle socks, swaying kilts, and let's remember the spats. When they marched by, I would actually see older people start to weep, for the sound of a bagpipes brings back many memories for people, including me.

Then came Dad's unexpected retirement from hockey in 1969, and 1970 was not a good year for the Cherry family.

Hershey Kisses streetlights in front of the Hershey Centre

Mom's sister Paulette and her husband
Richard Ferrante & me

Sunday, October 3, 2004
Woodbine Racetrack
Post Parade Room

8th Annual
Charity Golf Tournament

July 25, 2005
Glencairn Golf Club

A private reception with a
panoramic view of the world
renowned racetrack

Presented by

A Children's Hospice/Respite Centre

One of my proudest achievements

I think this was a posed picture for a newspaper.

Bobby Orr & Del at an IceDog game

SPOKANE COMETS .... AT HOME

LET'S PLAY THIS—Spokane Comet defenseman Don Cherry discusses the next musical selection with 5-year-old daughter Cindy under the watchful eye of Mrs. Cherry (Rosemarie) and the family pet, Ginger. This is latest in series on Spokane hockey players off the ice. (S-R photo)

My first puppy, Ginger

Somehow, I remember this house as being bigger.
Funny how that works.

Lft to Rt- Grandpa, his sister Hilda, Dad, his brother Richard, great-grandma,
grandma, Uncle Bill (Hilda's husband), Mom with me at my christening

When you measured snow by the foot, not inches.

Me & Jimmy McKenny @ a taping of the Grapevine show. Note: hooked rug which I did, and an old Amerk poster that Dad designed, both were stolen.

Me being the hockey mom with Del

Tie & Max Domi with Del, in the Leaf's dressing-room

Lacrosse buddies, Del & Max

Jim (Howie) McKenny & Tim in Rochester

Inside Cherry's Groomobile – Canada's first mobile dog grooming service.

Poolside fun

Dad showing off his many talents

Having fun with the base drum in his Scottish Pipe Band in Rochester

Full parade regalia in the hot summer

CHAPTER 13

WHAT A DIFFERENCE THREE YEARS MAKE

So how does Dad go from an unemployed, retired hockey player to coaching Bobby Orr in three years? In his first book, *Grapes: A Vintage View of Hockey*, he tells the story in great detail in the chapters "Comeback I" and "Comeback II." I'll give my version of the highlights.

Dad had missed a whole season of hockey. He'd been laid off from his job in construction and confirmed to himself that he was the world's worst car salesman. Yet with all this adversity, he had a vision of what he had to do for the rest of his life. He called the Amerk's office to speak to the GM and coach, Doug Adam. Do you know what the odds were of catching him in the office mid-summer? Not good. But Dad asked for a meeting, and lo and behold he got one. He was thirty pounds overweight but asked for a tryout for the coming season, and it was a go.

Dad's daily routine before camp would be to go up to our stifling hot attic and ride the stationary bike for hours. He'd put on sweats and wrap himself up in huge plastic garbage bags to heighten his sweating. He'd tighten the tension on the wheel so much you could smell burning rubber. Mom was so worried about him having a heart attack that she called his best friend Whitey Smith over to talk to him. His response was, "Yeah, that's right, I may die trying to make this club." He lost the weight and went off to training camp.

Here was a guy who had won three Calder Cups with this team, yet they treated him like a newbie at training camp. They gave him old gloves with holes in them and ripped socks and made him sit in the room with the rookies. They tried to break his spirit but did not succeed, no matter how hard they tried. He made the team, but little did he know this was a development team for Vancouver that could only dress three players over the age of twenty-five. He played well when they dressed him, but didn't play many games. It was heartbreaking to know Dad was being treated so disrespectfully.

Though I am thankful to Adam for giving Dad an opportunity, he lacked what it took to be an effective coach and a leader amongst men. He had many strange ideas and truly believed he was a disciplinarian. He was obsessed with the length of the players' hair, and that none were to have any facial hair. They were always to wear shirts and ties on the bus, and no beer was allowed on their long road trips. He wouldn't let them use curved sticks or drink soda pop. He hated rock music on the bus, so the players used to play the Rolling Stones and Led Zeppelin to bug him as he read his golf magazines. However, their favourite song to play was "Hair" by the Cowsills. The lyrics were brutal for a guy who hated long hair. The guys knew every word and sang it endlessly on the bus, driving him nuts. I must admit it is a catchy tune for such a clean-cut family singing group, and worth the listen.

The players had no respect for Adam and, worse yet, they cherished Dad. You can only imagine how this went over with the coach. While he was lecturing the team they would all look over at Dad for affirmation. It even got to the point that the coach himself would look over to Dad for approval. This guy had no control over the players and they hated him. It was so bad that one time a player came on the bus drunk and Dad made him sit in the back with him—he had a knife and Dad knew what he planned to do with it. Little did Adam know how close he came to being injured, or worse.

This all came to a head when they lost big at home. But first let me tell you what Adam did to Dad: he let him sit on the bench until the game's last five minutes. Then he threw him out on the wing, if you can believe it. All Dad thought was, *Please don't let me embarrass myself.* He got the puck, deked one way then the other, and put it in the top corner. He then skated as fast as he could to the bench and sat down. That was the last shift of his career.

The fans hated Adam so much that they attacked him after the game and threw beer in his face. It was apparent that he had lost the support of his team and fans. After the game, Dad went out for a few beers with his co-veteran teammate Bob Blackburn. A few turned into quite a few, and Dad got home very late. We started getting phone calls from management after eleven p.m., wanting to speak to Dad. Mom was embarrassed and said he wasn't home yet, so they called her every half hour till Dad came home around two a.m. He said it was too late to call them back, but Mom told him they said to call back whenever he came in that night. When he called, they wanted him to have a meeting at three a.m. Dad assured Mom, who thought this whole thing was ridiculous, that he'd be the Amerk's new coach when he came home. He was right, but unfortunately Adam was still the G.M. and Dad didn't get a pay raise, and they were at least eighteen points out of a playoff spot.

At this time Dad was still coaching his beloved Pittsford high school team, and they were going for the championship on the same day the Amerks were to play in Springfield. Not wanting to miss either game, Dad decided to meet the team in Springfield and let Adam go on the bus with the team. I remember him discussing this with Mom, both wondering if this was a mistake and whether he might have a mutiny on his hands. Without Dad controlling the team, who knew what they might do to Adam and the bus? She just shrugged, for she too was not a fan of this guy. Sure enough, it was a mistake. Not only was the music blaring, but they had a bonfire on the bus. The blaze was so out of control that they had to pull over and get the extinguisher to put it out. When Dad asked Adam what happened, all he was complaining about was the length of the goalie's and Bobby Walton's hair. That's how off his mindset and priorities were. By the way, Pittsford won the championship.

It came down to the last game of the season whether the Amerks would make the playoffs. They had to have a win; a tie would not do. The visiting team was the Cincinnati Swords, who had first place locked up, so this game meant nothing to them. The opposing coach was none other than Dad's buddy Floyd Smith. They had played together in Hershey, married local girls, and endured many seasons together in Springfield with Eddie Shore. Floyd also gave me my first teddy bear, which I kept for forty-five years. So, out of respect and friendship, Floyd started his backup goalie.

There are two major motivating factors in a goalie wanting to win: one is that he is going for a new contract the following season, and the other is when a coach starts you knowing the game is not important, or the coach doesn't really want to win the game. No doubt this goalie knew what was at stake, as well as the history between the two coaches. I know this because Dad applied this to his goalie Gilly Gilbert in Boston. If the team had been on a long and successful road trip, tired and probably going to lose the last game before heading home, he'd throw Gilly in net. If Cheevers was on a winning streak and due for a loss, he'd throw Gilly in. Dad had a different way of thinking than most coaches regarding who started in net. Most coaches go till the goalie loses then switches, but not Dad. He knew when he was pushing his luck with a winning goalie and would take him out on a high note. Then the backup would have something to prove, or, as in most cases with Dad vs. Gilbert, he'd win to spite Dad. The other motivating factor is whether the goalie is coming up to his contract year. There may be a third factor that may not be politically correct to say, but a French goalie likes to play well in Quebec. You may not think it's a factor, but it is.

As expected, this goalie stood on his head. The Amerks were leading 3 to 2 in the third period and outshot them 17 to 1. They scored on that one and only shot, and that was it for us. We needed that extra point, for we had equal points with Providence in the standings, but they had one more win than us. Adam was more than pleased to fire Dad, saying "we are making a change in your department." Dad thought for a moment and realized he was the only one in his department. As he was leaving the office, the secretary and public relations guy were snickering at Dad. Not being hockey people, they loved Doug Adam. As he left, Dad said, "You shouldn't chuckle at me that way. I'm like a bad penny: you never know when I'm going to turn up. Toodaloo." No truer words were ever spoken.

Once again Dad was out of a job with no prospects. Mom knew the hockey meetings in Montreal were coming up in the summer and wanted to know if Dad was going to go. She knew it was a place where hockey brass went with job offers in hand. Dad refused to go, saying he didn't want to look like he was begging for a job. That prompted the most vicious argument they ever had. Mom let him have it. He describes it well in *Grapes: A Vintage View of Hockey*, with Mom ending her tirade by saying, "We never have any money. Just you, that's all you can think of." He knew she was right, so out of desperation he called the GM of the Vancouver Canucks, Bud Poile. He replied, "If you were your brother, I would hire you. Sorry." *Click.*

Soon after he got a call from the owner of the North Carolina Checkers. Who knew there was a Southern Hockey League? (It folded in 1977.) Dad flew down to meet the brass and was interviewed by some Southern gentlemen. They asked him about his philosophy of hockey, the rudiments of coaching, the relativity of pucks, and transmediation. He went back to his hotel and contemplated his life. Why did he act the way he did? Why couldn't he cooperate with management? Was it really so bad that all Doug Adam wanted him to do was get the players to cut their hair? He was full of self-doubt, realizing he was 37 with a Grade 9 education and unemployed. He went to bed and cracked open a book to read, and a cockroach as big as his thumb ran across his chest. At this stage he knew there was one factor in his favour: things couldn't get any worse, so they had to get better. And he was right.

Three days later, the father of one of the boys Dad had coached at Pittsford High School called him up. He told him that he and seven other local businessmen had just bought the Rochester Americans and they wanted him to be coach. This was in the middle of the 1971–72 season. They offered him $15,000, the most money Dad had ever earned in a year, and he didn't even think of negotiating. Mom, the practical one, asked him who they were getting for GM. Dad didn't know, and she told him to call them right back up and tell him he'd be the GM for the same money. She figured he might as well, for she knew there would be no GM he could get along with. This sounded great, but the team came with one player, Dad, and the season was to begin in six weeks. (He was to be named GM the following year.)

1972 was the year the NHL expanded again and the WHA came into existence, so players were scarce. In all this excitement, what was Dad thinking of? Seeing the faces of that secretary and PR guy on his first day in the office. I can still remember him telling Mom he would make their life miserable and not fire them right away, because he wanted to see them suffer. Mom just shook her head and walked away. Dad always referred to this secretary (not directly) as "Syphilis." I knew her name was Phyllis, but I didn't know what syphilis was. I asked Mom one day why Dad called her that, and her reply was that Dad was an asshole. After that he never called her Syphilis again, but referred to her as "Dragon Lady." I can remember the new owners coming in and saying Phyllis was crying about the way he treated her. He asked how that could be, as he never talked to her. He completely ignored her, which drove her nuts. She eventually quit, for I could never see Dad firing her. They needed some sort of a secretary, so I was hired for the summer. I answered the phones, typed all the letters, did all the banking, kept track of season ticket holders, assisted in the marketing—I did it all, except dealing with players. I was even hired as the caterer for the press box. My first task, however, was to set up an aquarium in Dad's office.

I know it will seem harsh to some people that he was mean to his former secretary by not giving her the time of day, and it may add to the myth about Dad being misogynist, but let me explain about Dad and secretaries. I know they are now called "executive assistants," just as stewardesses are now referred to as "flight attendants." I have gone to many business meetings with Dad. When the boss would ask if we'd like coffee, we knew it was the secretary who was going to get it. I never saw Dad once take someone up on this offer. I always took his lead and also declined. I once asked him why he did this, for it seemed like a friendly gesture to break the ice. His reply surprised me, saying, "I think it's demeaning to her." This same philosophy was carried over to flight attendants. He hated asking for more coffee on a flight, so he'd set up poor Ron MacLean. If Ron was dozing off or entrenched in a book, Dad would mention to the attendant in a low voice, "I think Ron wants more coffee." She would come back with the pot, interrupt Ron, and ask him if he wanted more. He'd politely say please and thank you, and they would then ask Dad if he wanted more. His reply was always the same, "Well, since you're here," and he'd mumble something to her about Ron being so demanding. It was one of the many games they played against each other. So please, when you hear someone refer to Dad as "old school," "a misogynist," etc., remember these examples of how he respects women so.

After I returned to high school in the fall and hockey was soon to start, he hired a wonderful woman named Anita to hold down the fort in the office. She loved hockey so much that she played in a women's league—remember, this was the early seventies. She adored Dad and would do anything for him. I guess this was because he never asked her to get him coffee or lunch or get someone on the phone for him. He treated her with the utmost respect. One time he came in with a cold and she brought in homemade chicken soup for his lunch the next day. He appreciated it, for he usually just brown-bagged it and ate at his desk.

After Anita was on board, he hired a man named John Denhammer as a combination of public relations, general manager, and everything in between. He was the perfect guy for what Dad needed. That's all the staff they had in the front office for an AHL club. Dad operated on the shoestring budget the owners gave him and ran a tight ship. But oh, how John and Anita didn't get along. John would come into the office and yell, "Anita, coffee!" You could see her seethe. But Dad didn't help matters, sometimes fuelling the fire. I asked him one day, "Why do you do that? Don't you want the staff to get along for a smooth-running office?" He explained it in Cherry logic. He knew he wouldn't spend much time there and wanted to be kept in the loop. He figured if they had no mutual allegiance they'd squeal on each other and tell Dad everything that went on. One trip-up by either one and Dad would hear about it. He also applied this to the trainer, the assistant trainer, and the stick boy. This made total sense to me, and I marvelled at what a clever dad I had.

When Dad brought Blue into the office, we told Anita not to bend over to say hello to her as she may jump upward and break your jaw—nothing is harder than a Bull Terrier's head. Anyone who knows the breed knows how nutty they can be. There's nothing they do at half speed; it's all or nothing (meaning "couch potato"). John wanted to show Anita how well he knew Blue and called her into his office by clapping his hands. We yelled at him to stop clapping, but it was too late. She ran at him and jumped up on his desk, papers flying everywhere. She slid on the desk right onto his chest to kiss him. The chair flipped over and all we could see was his legs in the air. It was comical, but Dad and I were a bit worried for him. It made Anita's day.

Think about the pressure Dad was under. He had to put a team on the ice in less than five weeks. The only thing to do was hit the road, go to NHL training camps, see what players they didn't want, and go from there. His most significant break was from Denis Ball, one of the top brass of the NY Rangers. He sent Dad seven players who couldn't make their farm team in Providence. Even closer to the season, he offered to sell the player that Dad said he wanted from the very start, tough guy Bob Kelly, and Dad bought him for $7500.

There was no question that Dad would need a physical team, and with that came an entertaining brand of hockey. Rochester was always a hockey town, but with the rock 'em, sock 'em type of play that Dad produced, the fans came out in droves. The War Memorial Arena could seat 7000, but with standing room only they could get another 1200 in the building. That was until one of the owners told the fire marshal to move from the special seat along the boards that Dad had arranged for him. That was the end of any standing-room availability.

Dad's coaching skills were now coming to the surface from all the hardships and injustices he had endured as a player. Take, for instance, how he handled his tough guys. Bob Kelly proved himself to be an enforcer, but in the 1972-73 season he played 70 games, scored 27 goals, had 35 assists, and accumulated over 200 minutes in penalties. Dad explained to him that, once he got a reputation, he wouldn't have to fight as often. If anything, things would settle down when he took the ice. The newbies to hockey don't understand that kind of thinking. These are the same types that dreamt up the "instigator rule." I wanted to see what year this rule was put in, so I googled it. The response made me giggle at whoever writes the internet. It read, "Back in 1992, the NHL introduced a new rule that made non-fighting, cheap-shot artists rejoice with glee." It was "to protect superstars from getting picked on by tough guys," but it did the opposite. It was now open season on the stars, for no enforcer could protect them, like Semenko and McSorley did for Gretzky or Bob Probert for Stevie Yzerman.

Dad loved Bob Kelly like a son, and he would have liked to have kept him as long as he was the coach and GM of the Amerks. But he knew he had to be fair, and Bob belonged in the NHL. He had an obligation to the owners, so he made a few calls and sold Bob to St. Louis for $50,000—what an ROI! Halfway through their season St. Louis traded him to Pittsburgh, where he played four seasons. A week later we received a package with a colour TV from Bob and his agent, Charles Abrahams, with a note thanking Dad for what he did for his career. What a class guy. (P.S., the television went in my bedroom.)

One of the most memorable games Dad coached was when Providence came to town. Think about these dynamics: close to half of our team had been cut from Providence, the NY Rangers' farm team. Dad didn't need to tell them they were a team of misfits, for they knew. The motivation to win was there, and win they did. Can you imagine the conversation amongst the Rangers' management to be beaten by guys you didn't want? It reminds me of the 2017 "Golden Misfits" from Vegas that had something to prove when they made a run for the Stanley Cup.

Life was good in Rochester. The team always did well, and the fans came out to support them. The owners were happy because they were making money. A dealership gave us a car that was a driving billboard for the Amerks. The family even went on a free celebrity Hawaii trip and a cruise, with Dad being the celebrity. Mom and Dad even started a successful hockey school in the summer. He had seen how *not* to run one, and now it was his turn to do it right. He even hired some of his Amerk players as instructors. It was sold out in the first year, and they were set to hold it at a brand-new rink that was being built in Rochester. A cement strike happened and the rink didn't get finished, so they had to refund everyone's money. The second year was so successful that parents signed up for the following summer. Little girls also wanted to go to hockey school. Mom asked Dad what we should do and he didn't hesitate, saying they should be allowed to come, and he ensured the parents they would have separate dressing rooms. Again, Dad was before his time in being fair to women.

They also started a hockey school in their second year in Boston. How could it not be a success with the Boston Bruins coming out as instructors? Would you refuse if your coach asked you to teach at his hockey school?

Dad told me a story about Ricky Middleton coming out to be an instructor. He got in his car but it wouldn't start. He returned to the rink to get some of the guys, Dad included, to look under the hood. There was not a drop of oil in it and the engine had seized. He knew you had to put gas in it, but no one told him about the oil. Thank goodness he knew how to play hockey.

Dad received Coach of the Year in his third year of coaching in the AHL. We had roots in the community and were very content. Then the Boston Bruins came calling. He went from being an unemployed construction worker to coaching Bobby Orr in three years.

CHAPTER 14

THE KIDNEY TRANSPLANT

Y ou are only educated about specific health issues once they hit your family, as I now know all too well. I never gave kidney disease a second thought. My parents kept it that way until I returned to Boston after graduating from college in Kingston, Ontario, in 1978. I wanted to stay there, but I was on an American student visa and what worried the Canadian government even more about this alien in their country was that I had a four-year-old American car here. I wish I had kept all the letters I got from the government, as they were so amusing. I guess I was a threat to their economy and they wanted me out of the country. It came down to me receiving a registered letter stating that if I wasn't out of the country by September 1, 1978, my car would be impounded and who knows what they would do with me. I figured I'd better not push them too far and have to say goodbye to my boyfriend, grandmother, and great-grandmother. You can only imagine Dad's rant about all this. It had something to do with rowing a boat to Canadian shores.

When I got home to Boston and saw my brother, I couldn't believe my eyes. He was so pale. I then learned how essential kidneys are to our systems. Tim's were only working at 15 percent capacity, but he was alive and doing dialysis every other day. Of course it all fell on my mother's shoulders, for training camp was soon starting. Dad always admitted that he was not good at handling these crises and liked burying his head in the sand. He immersed himself in hockey, which was just as well, for Mom was the strong one and kept the whole family in check.

Being naive about kidney failure, I thought dialysis was a cure. I didn't know about options such as kidney transplants—they just never occurred to me. Mom was at her wits' end, driving into Boston two or three times per week and watching them struggle to hit my brother's veins, then hooking him up to a machine. You soon learn how amazing these organs are when you see how much effort a huge dialysis machine takes to do what a two-pound organ does.

Mom knew something else had to be done, for this was no life for a thirteen-year-old kid. She called a family meeting and said, "That's it, we're going to go for a transplant." It was a joint decision, and whoever was the best match would donate their kidney. I never really gave it much thought—it was just the thing to do. In my eyes, there was no bravery in it or any debate. I guess other people have different takes on it. Even the doctor, when telling me I was a perfect match to my brother, said some families don't move forward with it. I couldn't believe it! But that's us. We are not an overly affectionate family. We don't hug or say "I love you" every time we hang up the phone to one another, but when the chips are down we are there in spades.

Mass General in Boston is quite the hospital. It's number one in research and the third oldest hospital in the U.S., and of course it's the largest teachers' hospital of Harvard. John Wayne received a pig valve for his heart there around the same time. We missed being on the same floor as the Duke by only two weeks. I did get to see the majestic room he stayed in, and thought it was a room fit for the Queen of England. It had a huge fireplace and a bay window that overlooked the Charles River. The closest I got to him was meeting his nurse and seeing the coffee cup he gave her. I thought that was a really big deal at the time.

Some people have a real issue dealing with a teachers' hospital, with students coming around and talking about you as if you are their guinea pig, but I didn't mind at all. I had a pre-operational procedure to see what kidney they would take. It was done on an operating table with a local anesthetic going into the femoral vein in my thigh. The whole table was surrounded by students watching, and they asked me if I minded if another one of them tried to hit the vein and inject the dye. I said, "Sure, everyone has to learn." They had a mirror above the table so I could watch, but I couldn't see very well because I didn't have my glasses on. The next day they did the other leg and I wore my contacts. It was an amazing thing to see.

I agreed to let them use a new tactic in closing my long incision. To be sure the kidney they took out didn't get damaged in the process, they had to take out one of my ribs, which is why I ended up in so much pain from the operation. This new type of closure replaced stitches or staples, using instead a long, fine wire. They said the advantage of this was that it didn't leave a scar. When they went to pull it out in one big yank, it didn't budge. The doctor got frustrated and blamed me for waiting too long to get the wire out. The skin had grown around the wire so it was now embedded in me. It was the first time I had experienced beads of sweat from nerves. I told the doctor to just go for it, so he did. The pain was so extreme that I saw stars and got lightheaded. It felt like I was being sawed in half. I told them I highly recommended they didn't use this procedure again, and that I would have gladly taken the ugly scar, which after all that was still severe.

My brother got a private room, while I shared a room with a woman who had just had a baby. She was happy about it, but she was very sick. They had told her not to get pregnant, as her liver was failing, but she really wanted a family and went for it. She and I talked a lot, and what I liked about her most was that she didn't like TV, so I got to watch what I wanted. When I returned to my room after the operation, her bed was empty. I said to our nurse that I was glad she finally got to go home with the baby. In a matter-of-fact tone they told me she had died. I honestly didn't believe she was that sick, and the reality of what can go wrong in the hospital became apparent. I know that's what sometimes happens in hospitals, but I believe they shouldn't have put us together knowing she was that close to death.

Our operation was on the tenth of October 1978. I was in the hospital with one big happy family: Brad Park was in for his knee and Wayne Cashman for his back. When the game was on TV we'd all sit together and watch. For one game, the referee and linesmen came for a visit during the day. They gave me a collection of cassettes, for they knew the Bruins had given me a large portable cassette player. They asked if Dad would come back to visit after the game; I said I doubted it because visiting hours were over at nine p.m. They looked at each other and said, "Oh, we're sure he'll make it back in time." It was hilarious watching the game and seeing them waving off icings and offsides and not calling penalties. Even the announcers commented on the refereeing being quite good that night. It was probably one of the quickest games ever played at the Gardens, and I knew why.

This being the U.S., there was no socialized health care like in Canada. But even the American government realized that having a kidney transplant is so expensive that no insurance could cover it, due to two people being involved, so they paid for it all. Mom did, however, receive invoices for all the expenses. It was amazing how they kept track of every single item involved with us staying there, every bandage, needle, and medication, even our meals. I remember looking at the binders full of these charges—it was incredible. They even charge you for blood used if people didn't donate in your name. We found out by accident that not only did the Bruins donate blood, but their wives did too. We learned this in the wives' room before a game months later via Paula Schmautz complaining that she couldn't believe they wouldn't take her blood because she didn't weigh at least one hundred pounds. Oh, to have such problems.

The Bruins knew what Dad was going through, and though he wouldn't show them any emotion it took its toll on him. Before one game warm-up, he thought he'd have a quick power nap on the trainer's table. The players came in, dressed quietly, went out for their warm-up, and returned, all while Dad was napping.

While Tim was writing the movie script for Dad's bio, *Keep Your Head Up, Kid*, he came to my house one day while my son and I were playing ping pong. He said he was hitting a roadblock in writing the dialogue about his surgeon, Dr. Heron, in the section where he was telling us about the kidney transplant procedure and what to expect. It's not like in Canada, where the donor has to have physiological exams and it takes four to six months to set it up. Once our decision was made, it only took three weeks before Tim and I were wheeled side by side down the hall to the operating room. I can only imagine how Mom and Dad felt.

I told Tim I remembered the conversation vividly, for the doctor was very thorough even though it only lasted twenty minutes. I thought it was amusing that they didn't even make me sign a consent form. Years later, Tim ran into the doctor and asked why they didn't ask me to sign anything. His reply was great: "We knew who we were dealing with." After he explained what we could expect, he asked us if we had any questions. At the time none of us spoke up, and to tell you the truth I wanted to ask a semi-intelligent question to show him we were into it. But instead there was an uncomfortable silence from all of us. I remembered reading somewhere that, when people have their appendix or bladder removed, they lose a lot of weight, so our only question was from me: "How much weight will I lose?" He looked stunned and perturbed, and I could see that wasn't exactly the type of question he had expected. He gave me the unfortunate news: the best I could hope for was about a one-and-a-half-pound loss, the weight of the kidney, and I was truly disappointed.

I told Tim that this was all that was said during our one and only consultation before the big day. I doubted that CBC would want to put that in the script, since it's not very dramatic. When he ran it by them, though, there were women in the room who thought it was hilarious and loved the dialogue. So there it was, on TV for all the world to see: my issues with my weight. I can still remember being in the hospital with the IV in me complaining to the nurse to get it out. She asked me if it was hurting my hand and I said yes. I was too embarrassed to tell her I wanted it out because I figured if it wasn't in, I'd drop five pounds. I look back at that photo of me in the hospital bed and I only weighed about 125 pounds. It's too bad I couldn't have enjoyed that weight then. Just the other day I explained to my son what the quote "youth is wasted on the young" means. No cliché was ever more relevant than this one is to my time in that hospital.

The operation went well, but I can only imagine the thoughts going through my parents' minds when they saw their kids being wheeled to the operating room. Afterwards, Mom stayed in Tim's room while my boyfriend, who had flown down from Kingston, and Dad were with me. As I awoke, my first thought wasn't how Tim was, but why they had put the dozen roses they bought me close to the heating vent. I explained to them they would wilt quickly there, and asked them to be moved. Dad shook his head and said, "We thought you might say that, but we wanted you to see them as soon as you woke up." How well they both knew me.

That night, Tim walked down to my room to tell me I had to get up and walk around too. I was in a lot of pain and said, "No way. I want more morphine." Seeing his face flush without his previous paleness was so worth it. He was sliced in three places: twice where they took his kidneys out and once where my kidney was put in. Today they leave the old organs in and do the whole thing laparoscopically, including taking the kidney out from the donor. There's no slicing the donor from stem to stern like they did me.

Tim thrived afterwards. He needs no more dialysis, which is a godsend. I got myself a new job and was back working in about four weeks. We all counted our blessings, and to this day our family does what we can to promote organ transplants. Have you signed up to be a donor? Your organs are of no use to you when you're dead. Why people don't do this is beyond my comprehension. Is it selfishness or ignorance? Either one doesn't make sense to me.

CHAPTER 15

BEANTOWN TO ROCKY MOUNTAIN HIGH

A t the end of my junior year of school at East High in 1974, I had to say goodbye to all my friends because we were moving to Boston. To say this was a tough school would be an understatement. However, I had a clique of friends that I hung out with, and I am one of those rare people who say they really enjoyed high school.

A few years ago, I was at a function with Dad when some women came up to me and said, "We're from Rochester." When anyone says that I always perk up, for I have such fond memories of that city. I looked at them and said, "Are you ladies *really* from Rochester, or a surrounding suburb like Irondequoit or Pittsford?" They said, "Yeah, you're right, we're from Brighton." I told them I knew it, and they responded, "Yeah, like you guys lived in Rochester." The connotation here is that in the seventies, urban flight was peaking. I told them I went to East High and they stepped back, rolled their eyes, and said, "Really?" To prove my point, my New York statewide high school exams were cancelled the whole three years I went there due to riots. I knew my senior year in Boston would be a breeze.

You would think that, now we were going to the big time, it would come with a fancy house and such. Nope. The Bruins had a tiny house (about 1200 sq. feet) that they routinely rented from a couple who had moved to Florida for the winters. In Canada they are called "snowbirds." When Ron saw it on a segment of HNiC, he said, "Really? That's the house you lived in while you coached the Boston Bruins?" This was the house that newbies to the team would live in till they got their bearings and decided where they wanted to live. We stayed there for two years. It was within walking distance of my and Tim's school and had many places where I could get a part-time job after school. The problem was that it was not available when school started.

A scout for the Bruins lived close by, and he had a daughter my age whom I could live with for a month or so till Mom and Dad moved from Rochester. I was OK with this arrangement, but the girl certainly wasn't. Looking back, I can see her point. She was the big cheese in school, for her dad scouted locally for the Boston Bruins. Then I come in, the daughter of the new coach, which trumps a scout. One of the first nights I was there I drove all her friends to a school dance to kick off the school year. What do they do but start smoking joints in my parked car! To tell you the truth, I was more upset with them smoking in my car than it being illegal. Sure enough, a cop came and tapped on my window—you can imagine how scared I was. I rolled down my window and smoke billowed out. He looked at my orange NY plates and asked for my registration and driver's license. He took a look at my last name and all the references to New York and told me to smarten up, and welcome to Boston. I kicked everyone out of my car and drove home for the night. I never went out with her again. She was a social butterfly, and most nights I stayed home playing Yahtzee with her dad. My mom always asked me why I didn't go out with her more, and I just said, "She's too cool for me," and laughed.

I'll never forget the first Christmas there. Sure, there was always a skating party for the whole family at the Gardens, but the one with no kids is the most memorable for me. The night of the team party Mom and Dad came home with a Yorkie puppy wearing a knitted Bruin's sweater with "Blue" written on it. It was a tradition at these parties that gag gifts were exchanged, and so were hard feelings. For instance, Bobby Orr gave right winger Terry O'Reilly a pair of double runners—skates with two blades each for beginners. He didn't laugh. The trainer and his wife were given a picture of two obese naked people walking down a beach hand in hand, which caused embarrassment. Then Betty Cheevers, Gerry's wife, whose thumbs looked weird, received a pair of funny-looking fake thumbs—she was not amused. These gifts really hit a nerve with a lot of people. The first thing that came out of Dad's mouth as I played with the puppy was,

"We're not keeping it." He ended up giving it to his winger, Ken Hodge, and that was the end of gag gifts at the Christmas party.

The most memorable thing that happened that first year was how Dad reacted to the Bruins losing in the first round of the playoffs. In those days the first round was the best of three, and we lost to Chicago. When the Bruins blew them out of the water with a big score in the first game, the headlines questioned whether this was the end for their veteran goalie, Phil Esposito's brother Tony. Nothing motivates a goalie more than suggesting they should hang it up. Tony stood on his head as we outshot them three to one in the next two games, but they still won. We were all in shock. All I remember was Dad saying, "Those guys said they'd be ready."

When you look back at that scenario, at least half of that team had won two Stanley Cups in 1969-70 and 1971-72, guys like Esposito, Bucyk, Hodge, Doak, Cashman, and Marcotte, so when they said they'd be ready for the playoffs, Dad believed them. They knew what it took to go the distance, so Dad probably thought, *Who am I to question them?* Then the unimaginable happened: one player said in the paper, "We weren't prepared." When a player says that, it reflects on the coach. He was so upset he told Harry he'd understand if he fired him, and he wouldn't have to pay him for the remaining two years of his contract. Thank goodness Harry didn't, saying to Dad, "Coach like you did in Rochester and win, because if you don't we'll both be fired." Dad seethed, and that whole summer all we heard for music in the house was "Won't Get Fooled Again" by The Who. The last two lines about the new boss being the same as the old boss wasn't true in this case: he wasn't the same coach as in his rookie year. Just an FYI, the player who made the comment about not being prepared only played twelve games into the next season before he was traded.

You'd think he would tighten up the reins on the players, but it was exactly the opposite. For instance, management would make it mandatory to have a team meal at eight p.m. the night before a game on the road. Not only that, but they'd make them pay for it with their per diems. Dad never liked this himself, so he let them do their own thing the night before a game. They could eat and drink when they wanted to, but not in the hotel they were staying in. Plus, as with the way he raised his kids, there was no curfew. Dad would never lay down the law to any newcomers to the team. What would happen is a veteran like Wayne Cashman or the captain would tell them that they had a good thing going with Don, and just not to cross him. Tim and I learned this as children, and his players soon realized the same. What would happen if someone took advantage of his good nature? Here's an example.

One of Dad's favourites, Bobby Schmautz, got hammered the night before a game. Worse yet, at breakfast the next day he accidentally broke a crepe pan. You have no idea how this is a big no-no for Dad. He felt how his players acted in a hotel, on a plane, anywhere in public, was a true reflection of him. So now everyone wanted to see the repercussions he was going to inflict upon his favourite player for the afternoon game in Minnesota. Was he going to bench, fine, or suspend him? Nope, he played him to death. With a severe hangover, Bobby took a regular shift, killed penalties, and worked the power play. He came back to the bench puking, barely able to skate. I know this because Tim was the stick boy for that game. As he was throwing up on the bench, Bobby said to Tim, "How you doing, Tim my boy?" Even the players said to Dad, "You're going to kill him." Dad's reply was, "Let him die." Yikes. He threw him in on the last shift of a tied game. He deked, dove, and scored, then slid into the boards and laid there. Even the broadcasters said he must have been injured, as he wasn't moving. The players rushed out, looking like they were congratulating him for the game-winner, but they really wanted to haul him up from the ice and drag him back to the bench. Remember, Bobby is one of Dad's best friends on and off the ice. He played for Dad in Rochester, Boston, and Colorado. He even installed a new roof for us in the summer. But when Dad wants to make a point, everyone's at risk.

Another tradition that the Bruins had that Dad eliminated was hazing. Throughout his career he had seen awful things happen to players in this ridiculous ritual. He witnessed broken arms and legs resulting from the players fighting back. He often said he thought Ron Duguay lost the title of 1977 Rookie of the Year with the NY Rangers because they shaved off all his curly golden-blond locks. As a player he never participated in them, but he never intervened either. So when he was made coach all of it stopped, except one time. For multiple reasons, Dad didn't like one particular rookie, and he let him suffer this stupid childish ritual. Once again, it doesn't pay to get in Dad's bad books.

The previous coach also made them have a team meal on the day of a road game. Again, Dad knew the players didn't like this. They all have their preferences of when they want to eat and take a nap on the day of a game. Some like eating before their afternoon nap, and others like it afterward. So, once again, they could do what they wanted. That is why he was called a "players' coach." He thought like a player and realized they were all individuals, plus he remembered the things he didn't like as a player. For instance, he never weighed the players; his philosophy was: as long as they win, who cares? However, this kind of thinking does not go well with upper management. Some short-sighted people might have though he didn't have control of his players, which as you can see is not the truth. These questions are all about job security. Do you worry about the perception of your coaching style, or, as in Dad's case, do you ignore the norm?

The country-club attitude that many of them had in the first year Dad took over soon disappeared, and so did many of those players. In the next four years they finished in first spot in the Adams Division, went to the finals twice, and went to the third round twice. Plus, in 1976, Dad won the Jack Adams Award for Coach of the Year.

I went to most of the games during high school. Sometimes I drove down to the Gardens myself, usually for Saturday afternoon games. I wanted to get home early to go out at night with my friends. Like in his playing days, Dad was always the last to leave the dressing room. Some things never change. I couldn't park inside the Gardens like Dad did, so I used the public lot down below. Before the season's last game I announced in the wives' room that I was to be congratulated, for my spoke-wheel hubcaps did not get stolen the whole season—what a feat! Those hubcaps were a big deal in the seventies; they were very expensive and I cherished them so. Sure enough, after that game they were all gone. I was upset and Dad, in his never-sympathetic way, said, "That's what you get for not going to the game with us." However, Dad being Dad, he went to Frosty Forristall, who was not only the Bruins' trainer but a "fixer." Miraculously, these same hubcaps were put back on my car during the next home game.

After one Saturday afternoon game, I was trying to get out of the Garden's parking lot. There was to be a Celtics game that night, and that crowd was very different. You can imagine the traffic jam. As I was trying to turn left onto the main street, no one would let me into the intersection. Then I felt my car moving, even though my foot was on the brake—the truck behind me was pushing me. Thankfully my Monte Carlo had a huge bumper. Can you imagine if they tried that with today's cars? As I was about to hit a vehicle in the street, its driver looked at me and I pointed behind me. He put his car into park, got out, and got into a fight with the guy behind me. They fell onto the trunk of my Monte Carlo, and I took off. I was so upset that I was still home when Mom and Dad arrived, and they asked me why I didn't go out. I told them about my harrowing experience. I don't remember Mom being concerned at all but Dad shook his head—his main concern was not for me, but the car. He told me again: that's what you get for not coming down to the game with us. Plus, if going out at night is so important to me, I'd better be prepared to suffer the consequences. If you're looking for sympathy when you do something stupid, don't look to Don Cherry.

I graduated from from East High School in Rochester, New York, and Saugus, Massachusetts in 1975. After going to all the graduating hoopla in Saugus, I returned to Rochester and went to all their functions too. A teacher came up to me and said, "I didn't see much of you this year," and I replied that I took a lot of bird courses and stayed under the radar.

After graduating from high school, I decided to go to post-secondary in Kingston. Usually if one says they went to school in Kingston, its assumed it was to Queen's University. I chose to go to the community college there, St. Lawrence. Dad's only comment was that he couldn't believe people from all over the world came to go to school in Massachusetts, so I decided to leave it. Looking back, I can see the point he was trying to make. I could have experienced the next three years going to the games and enjoying Boston to its fullest. I did have fun going to the games when he played Toronto and Montreal, though, as Kingston is right in the middle of these two cities. And yes, I was there on Feb. 7, 1976, when the Leafs' Darryl Sittler had his famous ten-point game against the Bruins, with six goals and four assists.

Everything was going against the American-born Dave Reece, who was in goal that fateful night. The Bruins were on a seven-game winning streak at the time, and Gilly Gilbert was injured. It was also Gerry Cheevers' first game back from his three-and-a-half-year hiatus with the Cleveland

Crusaders of the World Hockey Association, so there was no way Dad would start him. What logic would there have been for Dad to throw Gerry to the wolves on his first game back with the Bruins? There was no question that the Bruins were due to end their streak. Dad has often said that sometimes you know you are not going to win a game, and this was one of them. Also, a lot of players were from around that area, and their minds were on seeing relatives and not on the game. It was also on HNiC and being broadcast across the country.

So in goes poor Dave Reece. While he's being hammered, Dad gave a slight look down the bench to Gerry, who had just put a towel over his head. There was to be no mercy pull for poor Dave, and that was his last NHL game. Hockey is not only a tough sport, but unfair in so many ways.

I'd stay with Dad at the Westin and go to his room before going to the Gardens for the game. Before leaving one day, he said, "Oh, I almost forgot the beer." He got on a chair and removed some ceiling tiles, revealing a case of beer. He told me that was why he always got that suite, so he could keep his stash up there, as room service was very expensive. He also wanted it cold when he got back to the room, so he put it in the toilet tank. No question, when it comes to getting the beer cold he is one clever fellow. He would put beer in a pillowcase and hang it outside the bus window to keep it cold on long road trips in the minors. It's true what they say: necessity is the mother of invention.

One time I arrived early from Kingston to meet Dad at his hotel. He was about to take his afternoon nap before the game, and told me to go to a particular store, where they would be waiting for me. He was excited to tell me he had bought me a full-length raccoon coat and I had to get fitted for it. I had to hurt his feelings and seem like an ungrateful child when I said, "Thanks, but no thanks." It was amusing to hear him call them up and say his daughter was one of those kooks who wouldn't wear fur. Remember, this was the seventies and the political correctness of not wearing fur wasn't in full swing like today. Nowadays I wouldn't even wear a coyote-fur-hooded Canada Goose jacket if you paid me.

When the Bruins would charter a flight to Montreal or Toronto, I would sometimes fly back with them, usually around Christmas and March break. Some of the players would come up to me and say, "Cindy, let me carry your suitcase. Maybe your dad will put me on the power play."

As usual the Bruins ended up in first spot that year, but playoff hockey is a totally different game. I asked Dad once why teams don't play like they do in playoff hockey for the rest of the season. His answer surprised me: players can't play full out every game for the whole season like they do in the playoffs. I asked if they paced themselves during the season, to which he said, "It's just a different game." I guess it's hard to describe, but if you are a hockey fan you know it's a different level of play.

There are normal sports fans, and then there are fans who live and die by the game. We Cherrys live in the latter world. The outcome of these series determines if you will be moving or not, even if you have a couple of years to go in your contract. If Dad wins the Cup, how can Harry Sinden fire him? If he loses, it's fodder for the perfect reason to get rid of him. In the final year of his contract their relationship had deteriorated to non-communication. It even came to the point that the team and Dad stayed in a different hotel than Harry and assistant GM Tom Johnson. The semi-finals with Montreal of that year can be summed up by three words: "too many men." This series was the de facto Cup finals, as the winner went on to the finals to meet the NY Rangers, which should have been a breeze to the Stanley Cup.

On May 10, 1979, we were leading Montreal by one goal at the Forum with 2:34 left in Game 7 of the Stanley Cup semifinals. Linesman John D'Amico called too many men on the ice against Dad, which was indisputable. My heart sank for Dad, for when this call is made the cameras zero in on the coach. Guy Lafleur scored on the ensuing power play to tie the game. Midway through sudden death, as it's appropriately called, Yvon Lambert scored and it was over.

I was sitting at home with Mom watching the game. We just sat in silence when that goal was scored. This was more than just losing a game, this was knowing big-time changes in our lives were coming up. There was no question: our time in Boston was up.

Dad had an impressive résumé: four first-place finishes, Coach of the Year in both the AHL and NHL, and only two losses in the finals. So who comes calling but the Colorado Rockies. He met the GM, Ray Miron, and sealed the deal on a handshake that made Dad the highest-paid coach in the NHL. With no actual contract in hand, Dad's agent Al Eagleson called Dad up. He told him Leafs' owner Harold Ballard was offering more money and a longer-term contract. Plus, the Leafs were just a player or two away from the Stanley Cup, and my grandmother was only a three-hour drive away. Tempting as it was, he told Eagleson he was a man of his word and passed. Without a signed contract Eagleson couldn't believe he passed this up, but as a family we knew Dad was a man of his word.

Mom and Dad had to sell their beautiful house and find a new abode in Denver. I was at a crossroads in my life, too. I had finished college in Kingston, returned to Boston, and had the kidney transplant, but what was my big picture in life? I decided to fly out with them that summer while they searched for a house. While there, Mr. Miron and his wife graciously had us over for dinner. They talked incessantly about their poodle, as they thought we loved dogs. They showed us a book the team gave them as a Christmas gift, titled *Everything I Know About Hockey* by Ray Miron. When you opened it up, the pages were all blank. They thought this was hilarious. We looked at it in disbelief. It showed us how out of touch they were not to be insulted. After meeting them I knew Dad had no chance of getting along with this guy, and the challenges he would face were going to be immense. I knew I loved Kingston and all it had to offer. I had relatives, good friends, and my boyfriend there, so north is where I wanted to be.

However, returning to Canada was not as easy as I thought. I had gone to college there as an American student. Now I wanted back in, and the government said, "Not so fast." (Remember, it was the seventies.) I asked them what I needed as an American to get in. First I had to prove I had blood relatives in Canada, which was no problem. Then I had to have $25,000 in a Canadian bank account: done. I had to have a certified letter stating that I had a job waiting for me that no one else in Canada could fill. That was also provided. The outcome? Denied! Can you imagine what my dad had to say about that? Too bad the left-wing media couldn't get a tape on that—he would have been shot at dawn. No worries, though: I got my Canadian citizenship because Dad was born in Canada.

Before the season started in Colorado, Mom gave Dad something to think about: would he be able to come to terms with the idea of having a losing record the first couple of years until he assembled the team he wanted? He realized this when he showed Mom the team he would be coaching that year. Her comment, said in the most sincere way, was, "They look like a nice bunch of boys." Being used to the big, bad Bruins, the Rockies did look like a sweetheart of a team.

Starting at training camp, Dad and Miron clashed. Dad wanted to put together a winning team and the GM was worried about looking good to Armand Pohan, stepson to the owner, Arthur Imperatore Sr. Little did Dad know at the time that this New Jersey businessman, who had bought the team in 1978, had full intentions of moving the team to New Jersey when the construction of the Meadowlands Sports Complex was complete. Here are some examples of career-limiting moves by a coach, and Dad clashing with the G.M.

At training camp Dad sent down Miron's first-round pick, Mike Gillis, to Fort Worth, after he had been signed for big bucks. Dad knew he was floating through training camp and wanted him gone while he kept a hard-working player named Ron Delorme. This did not go over well with the owners and made Miron look bad.

The season before Dad got there, Miron signed a Swedish goalie named Hardy Astrom for big bucks who had played a whopping four games in the NHL. Dad nicknamed him the "Swedish Sieve." Dad wouldn't play him and started another goalie, Bill McKenzie from St. Thomas, Ontario, who was also in the organization—his season started with a 9–12 record with a pretty good goals-against average. But once again, when a coach isn't playing the top-paid players, the general manager looks questionable in the eyes of the owners. This ended when Dad headed into the Boston Gardens for his first game back. John Wensink, who played for Dad in both Rochester and Boston, slid into McKenzie and wrecked his knee, and the Swedish Sieve played the rest of the season.

You can imagine the hoopla with Dad's first return to Boston, much to the chagrin of the Bruins' management. I would venture to guess there probably wasn't a full-out effort by the Bruins to win that game. Their new coach, Freddy Creighton, probably knew this, so he threw Gil Gilbert in net, who had no love lost for Dad. Gilbert had every right not to like him—he was always the sacrificial lamb to go into net when Dad had an inkling they'd lose. If they won five straight out of six, Gilly would no doubt start in net. The team, Dad, and Gilly knew exactly the strategy here: to protect Cheevers at all costs. So who could blame Gilly for not liking Dad? Despite him being in net, the Rockies won 5–3.

Dad rarely called time-outs, but he did during this game for some reason. He said it was to give the team "a breather." What happened next you will never see again during an NHL game: Dad saw a kid at the end of the bench wanting his autograph, and he obliged. Everyone rushed to the bench, and suddenly he had a line-up of autograph hunters. He said he didn't do it on purpose and just felt bad for the kid, but if you wanted the Bruins' management to be ticked off, that would be the way to do it.

Want another instance of a career-limiting move by a coach? A local Denver paper published a survey asking if Don Cherry should be fired. About 3800 said no while 52 said yes. Dad's reaction was put in the article: "I didn't think Ray Miron had that many friends."

An incident with Dad and defenseman Mike McEwan, a favourite of the owners, sealed his fate with the Rockies. Dad liked short shifts, and McEwan was forever staying on the ice too long. During a game in Chicago he stayed out too long and the Blackhawks scored the winning goal. When he returned to the bench, Dad grabbed him by the sweater and shook him. McEwan then went M.I.A. on the team. It's reported he flew to New Jersey to meet with the owners about this incident. To get him back playing, they probably assured him Dad would be gone at the end of the season. Years later, when Dad was doing play-by-play with Danny Gallivan up in the gondola, he kept hearing a woman really giving it to him, and finally turned around to see who it was. It was McEwan's wife, and all Dad said was, "Isn't it just like Mike to get you the cheap seats." Ouch!

With the writing on the wall, everyone knew Dad would be fired at the end of the season, although it wasn't official until six weeks afterwards. A little-known fact is that attendance at the games that year increased by 150,000. Their final home game was a fitting farewell to Dad. Denver was amid a blizzard that night, yet 12,000 fans made their way to McNichols Arena to see the Rockies play Pittsburgh. Dad came out to start the game wearing a cowboy hat and boots. The players formed two lines and crossed their sticks in an arch for Dad to walk through. They won their final home game, beating the Penguins 5–0.

When you are fired after the first year of a three-year contract, you hope they will still pay you, and the debate began in court. Mom and Dad decided to stay in Denver until Tim finished high school in two years. In the meantime, Ralph Mellanby, the executive producer of HNiC, asked Dad to fly back east and do the colour for a few games, hatching his new career in broadcasting. He flew back and forth from Denver to Toronto for two years. When Tim graduated, it was time for them to head back east. What was the reason he gave to the press for leaving Denver? "I can't get used to watching Johnny Carson at 9:30 p.m."

With no place to live, they stayed the summer at the cottage on Wolfe Island, a ferry ride from Kingston. My grandmother and I were sure glad to have the family reunited. However, the cottage was no place to live in the winter, so they had to find a house somewhere in Toronto. Back and forth they drove, looking at houses. It got so frustrating that Dad was getting fed up, so for each potential house Mom and I would take the train up, peek at it for two seconds, and know it wasn't the one. Having been a real estate broker at one time myself, I find this is the problem with realtors: they don't listen to their clients. Sure enough, these realtors showed Mom and Dad one house that they instantly knew they didn't want. However, there was a house for sale right behind that one, and they asked to see it. The agents told them they wouldn't like it, and you guessed it: that was Mom's dream home in Mississauga.

CHAPTER 16

BOXES OF SUCCESS

*A*fter being fired by the Colorado Rockies and having a reputation for being unable to get along with management, it was uncertain times for Dad. Life is a journey for everyone, and we all have our challenges. One test of success in meeting these challenges is how well you rebound when life throws you a curveball. Now he had found himself out of hockey, neither as a player or a coach. What to do?

It was about this time that Dad met a person who would play a huge part in his life: Gerry Patterson. Gerry was a savvy sports agent and businessman, and a good friend of Ralph Mellanby's. Gerry Patterson became Dad's agent, and he was ahead of his time. He was a positive thinker and a visionary with goal-oriented tasks. He was the first person I knew who utilized a well-organized day planner. It was filled to the brim with essential dates and meetings, goals and daily challenges, ideas, and, most of all, motivational quotes, and your basic phone numbers and addresses. The most important thing I have to say about him is that he was a really good guy. Dad calls his type "salt of the earth," honest and trustworthy to a fault. So much so that we would get frustrated with how much of a trusting soul he was in this world of opportunists. We would warn him about certain people but he'd always see the good in them, and sure enough they'd end up suing him or worse. It was hard for Dad not to constantly say, "I told you so." He was always in a good mood and laughing. If you watch old videos of the *Grapevine* shows, you'll often hear a familiar loud laugh—that's Gerry's.

We have never sued anyone over lies and misrepresentations they have made regarding Dad. Take for instance this unbelievable story. It was always an urban myth that Dad owned one of the most ostentatious white mansions on Mississauga Road. A well-known, high-profile realtor in Mississauga and Ritchies Auctioneers advertised, "Don Cherry's Former Residence up for 8 Million Dollar Auction."[17] This 10,500 square foot palace had twelve bathrooms, nine fireplaces, a piano room, a Renaissance-inspired master bedroom with pink walls, and a gold four-poster bed. This palace was so well known I can remember Mom coming home from shopping one day all upset about a conversation she had with a lighting salesman. She was in his store, and he said how disappointed he was that she wasn't loyal to him because she had bought a huge chandelier for her foyer from someone else. She realized he thought she lived in this monstrosity of a building and had to convince him she didn't live there. The houses that the Cherrys own are not monuments to money. I can say this, for it came out of the mouths of babes. It was always funny listening to the trick-or-treating kids at Halloween when Dad was handing out candy. When they saw it was Don Cherry, they would routinely say, "You live here?" Dad always used to say the day after Halloween, "My house sure takes a shit-kicking. I don't know what people expect."

I found out this realtor was advertising this event only when a *Toronto Star* reporter called me and asked what I thought of my dad auctioning off his house and all its contents. It truly sounded like a bankruptcy fire sale, for this reporter told me the ad also referred to "a fine selection of jewellery, watches, designer handbags and a Ferrari 599GTB." I was stunned and the reporter knew it, and asked why I didn't know about it. Dad wasn't all that upset, but I was infuriated. He said, "You know everyone thinks I lived in that house," and he joked about it on Twitter. I wanted to go after this guy's real estate license, but all Dad did was call up his lawyer. All he had to do was knock off saying it was Dad's former place. In true Canadian fashion, he sent us an email saying sorry, which was the end of it. Every time I see his billboards and for-sale signs I seethe, and would love to tell

---

[17]   Canada, Huffington Post. "Don Cherry Denies Owning $8-Million Mississauga Mansion up for Auction (UPDATED)." HuffPost, 5 Aug. 2014, https://www.huffpost.com/archive/ca/entry/don-cherry-denies-owning-8-million-mississauga-mansion-up-for-a_n_5651276

his customers about his ethics. So please, when reading about the Cherrys, put your skeptic hat on and remember this book is ground zero regarding facts about us, and take everything else with a grain of salt.

When Gerry and Dad had their first meeting, his first order of business with Dad was to draw the next twenty years of his life in boxes. Each of the boxes in this diagram held part of a strategy. Each way of making money would lead to other things. In Dad's book *Sports Heroes*, he shows this diagram and explains how Gerry orchestrated all the boxes so they would come true. He believed in Dad, even when Dad questioned himself on Gerry's vision for his future.

The first of Gerry's boxes were banquets, a.k.a. the "rubber chicken circuit." Gerry drove Dad in his old four-door diesel Mercedes all over Ontario, and Dad perfected his storytelling persona. As soon as Dad would go off-script, as in telling his opinion about something, Gerry would lecture him all the way home. Nobody wants to hear about your philosophy of life and its lessons—stick to your hockey stories. This was so true. In the next box was written, "Radio Show." When Dad came home from taping his first five radio shows, he said to Mom, "I don't know how long I can keep this up. I may run out of stories." After at least 4200 shows and 35 years of *The Grapeline Show* with Brian Williams, heard coast to coast on at least a hundred radio stations, he never did run out. They even used to do a two-hour live coast-to-coast phone-in show that went on for years. Brian fondly remembered calls from "a farmer out in the fields on his tractor in Southern Manitoba, and another came from a family on the Alaska Highway. Young, old, male and female, all so happy to speak with Don." It was his call to end it in the summer of 2019, and boy, was that well-timed.

The next box had "TV" written in it, so the show *This Week in Hockey* was born. Remember, this was the eighties when sports were not analyzed to death—no internet, podcasts, SportsNet, TSN, ESPN, etc. Seeing highlights of the games played that week on regular TV was enlightening and enjoyable, but it was a lot of work to produce and script. Looking back, it was such simpler times: no one asked who actually had the rights to those highlights to make money off them. Could it be the owners of the team, the NHL, broadcasting stations, or the Players' Association? No one knew or asked. Nowadays everyone has their finger in the pie for rights, which is one of the reasons they had to stop making the *Rock'em Sock'em* highlights DVDs. *This Week in Hockey* was a fast-paced show, truly something to be proud of, and ahead of its time. It was about that time that Gerry, who was an entrepreneur extraordinaire, said, "You know what would be a great show? People sending in their home videos and showing them on TV." Little did he know. When I saw *America's Funniest Home Videos* debut in 1989, I chuckled. He certainly was a visionary.

This Week in Hockey led to the development of *Don Cherry's Grapevine*. Both were produced by Gerry's company, Special Events Television, and his business associates. This thirty-minute show had it all: comedians, singers, highlight clips of the guest, and the guest being interviewed by Dad. Mom often called up the stars to see if they'd like to be guests on the show. They'd barely get paid but got a cartoon sketch of themselves by the late Canadian artist Rob McDougall, plus a VHS tape of the show to take home. Most of the players brought their families. They knew it was a safe environment, and trusted that Dad was not one of those "investigative journalists." Most knew the questions ahead of time. This was the premise of his *Sports Heroes* book, which tells the inside stories of the guests on the show.

The program was filmed in a makeshift bar in the old CHCH studio in Hamilton, Ontario. To make it look real they had models as waitresses serving people pop at the table, then they stood at the bar looking pretty. So few people were in attendance that Mom and I had to sit in the audience to make it look natural. Sometimes the next guest would sit in the audience also, like Shawn O'Sullivan, a gold medalist in boxing at the World Amateur Championships and the light middle-weight silver medalist at the 1984 Summer Olympics. He sat with Mom and me, and we devoured the chips they put on our table, along with the pop. We asked if he'd like some and he politely declined: "I'm in training and all I've had today is an apple." We felt bad and told them to take the chips away.

We watched him fight in Toronto from ringside seats. I had never been to a live boxing match, let alone ringside. I soon learned it was like sitting too close to the glass at a hockey game: you see stuff you wish you hadn't. I couldn't get over what I thought were welts on Shawn's back. I told Dad I didn't think he had gotten hit enough to cause that much redness. Dad enlightened me that those were rope burns. By the fight's end they were raw, oozing blood, and oh-so painful-looking. That was my first and last live fight.

It was about this time that everyone kept asking us where the bar was. That was Gerry's next endeavour: restaurants. It was a natural progression, so on the hunt we went. Gerry found a business partner and we went all over the GTA and Hamilton area, searching for that certain place. Dad saw nothing he liked until we headed to an old deserted restaurant right down from the CHCH studio where the *Grapevine* show was taped. There was something about it that Dad got a feel for. When we checked it out, it still had plates, silverware, and salt and pepper shakers on the tables. There was old soup with ladles in it on the stoves. It looked eerie, something out of a movie. Gerry and his business partner said no way. For some reason, Dad saw the potential in this place and put an ad in a small local newspaper for a restaurant manager. That's how he met his new restaurant partner, Rick Scully, and the rest is history.

They developed this dilapidated building into a gold mine that was never again duplicated throughout the years. It was a dance bar Thursday, Friday, and Saturday nights, with lineups around the block. It had a strict dress code, with a DJ who knew how to work the floor. The other nights it was a sports bar with pay-per-view events and much more. It was a well-oiled machine, and I worked the bar. It was there that I learned what it takes and how easy it is not to be successful in the restaurant industry. I contribute this all to Rick, who was very clever and knew all the tricks in this world that was new to us.

Successful restauranteurs think differently, and it's the details that make or break you. I had several conversations with him that proved this point. I said, "Undoubtedly, we have the worst-tasting coffee in the world." He smiled and said, "Yes, we sure do. Why do I want people who have had their dinner and dessert to hang around with one cup of coffee? I want turnover on those tables, and letting them hang around with their third free refill of coffee doesn't make sense." I had never thought of it that way, and it made perfect sense. Plus, although I knew he wouldn't say it to me, it keeps your staff from drinking it by the gallon.

One day he yelled at me for wasting straws. I guess he felt comfortable yelling at me in front of staff for all to hear—if he could yell at the owner's daughter, all should heed his warnings. I did have a habit of putting one straw in a diet pop and two in a regular pop if I was serving them together. He explained to me how much those extra straws add up. So to distinguish them, I started putting lime on the diet. Then I got a lecture on the cost of fruit in the winter. I still think of him today when I get served water with a straw. At least now we think about it for environmental reasons, but back then it was purely the economics of it all. Plus, don't even think about putting a lemon with it unless they ask for it. We never ordered short cocktail straws, we just cut the fatter straws in two. One time I accidentally cut the thinner straws in two and got a theory on how that was wrong too: drinks go down faster through fatter straws. Makes sense to me!

It still amazes me how many people buy into a bar or restaurant and don't know what they're doing. You'd think when people purchase a franchise that had an existing recipe for success, as ours had when we sold it, they'd listen. I was always astonished at how rookie owners tried to buck our system. I questioned one owner why he would have dance music blaring in the middle of the week when a Leafs game was on. Even when we sold the three restaurants we personally owned, the new owners changed everything. In Hamilton, the first thing the new owners did was ease up on the dress code on the three big nights, making it so you could wear a ripped black t-shirt and ball cap and still get in. They didn't understand that this brought in a different element. Women who got dressed up to go dancing wouldn't want to mingle with this crowd. Once the women stop coming in and you have a tough crowd with no dancing, sales go down, so it dies a slow death. But in their eyes, we did everything wrong and they knew it all. I worked there after they took over, and their big new rule was that bartenders couldn't keep their purses under the bar. They thought we would steal from them that way.

We then sold our second personally owned restaurant in Mississauga. Dad asked me to stay on for a while to assist the owner. He didn't realize that most new bar owners thought they knew it all and we were big dumdums. He was perturbed when I quit suddenly, but he understood when I explained this following scenario. I played hostess, busboy, service bartender, expeditor of food, waitress—you name it, I did it to give good service. One day we were swamped. I was trying to keep things under control, but service was backed up and there was a lineup at the door. I looked at the bar, and who was eating a big bowl of pasta with sauce dripping down his face but the new owner. That was my last day working there, and once I explained that scenario to Dad, he just said, "Got it." One thing about Dad: if you explain things to him logically, nine times out of ten he will see the light. He has no problem admitting he is wrong if you come at him without antogonism, but with a clear argument.

I could write another book on why restaurants fail. I had a friend who was considering opening a restaurant who asked me for advice. First I told her, "Don't let waitstaff void their own mistakes," and second, "Know how to steal from a bar, for if you don't, the staff will rob you blind." One good trick is to let someone who you think is stealing do a manual inventory. To set them up, you'd think you'd make it so you'd be missing one case of beer, but what you do is add a case and see if they catch it. Most say, "Yeah, it's all there," never, "Gee, the numbers show we have an extra case." Another trick I thought I came up with on my own, but I was told that most smart restauranteurs do it, use clear garbage bags. A lot of stuff goes out the back door masquerading as garbage.

With the restaurants in full swing, a decision was made to film the *Grapevine* show in our actual bars. The concept was that the audience would be made up of people who had reservations for a nice dinner before the taping of at least two shows. Sometimes the guests of the show would have dinner with their families and then get ready to be interviewed as their guests watched. How unique is that?

One time we had to delay filming, and when Dad asked what the holdup was I had to tell him we were running behind because of dinner. He laughed and commented on how our priorities had changed.

Dad had to do an opening monologue about the guest for that night. They tried to keep it short but getting it right on tape was difficult. The producer suggested that, rather than talk to the camera and audience, he should pretend to be talking to Blue. They put a picture of her on the bar, and the rest is history. He felt a lot more comfortable, and telling Blue all about the guest that night flowed nicely.

It was a tight crew and they all looked out for Dad, but they didn't stop short of playing a few tricks on him. The one I remember most really got to him. In his dressing room before the show, he'd go over what he was going to talk about with either the producer or floor manager. One night there was an ex-Leaf in the crowd whom Dad wasn't too fond of, and he started on a spiel about him. It had something to do with the back of a barn and the colour of a duck's foot. When Dad came upstairs, they took him to the kitchen and told him they had a problem: the mic was on and the player had heard every word Dad said. The colour left Dad's face and he felt really bad. It was all we could do to keep straight faces, and then we started laughing. He called us a few choice words then went on to the show.

It was a well-produced episode. It opened with Dad getting dressed to ZZ Top's "Sharp Dressed Man," with clips of his coaching, great hits by the Bruins, John Wensink challenging the opposing team's bench, unbelievable goals, Formula One crashes, bull riding, boxing knockouts . . . it had everything. The closing was just as entertaining, with all the action pacing to the song "Na Na Hey Hey Kiss Him Goodbye." It had clips of unbelievable goals (check out Middleton's and Schmautzy's), mid-ice hits, Bobby's famous goal, Gretzky hoisting the cup, the glass shattering, Dad in true form behind the bench, a couple of Terry O'Reilly's fights, and, of course, it had to show a bit of the infamous Jonathan-Bouchard fight. Where Metro-Goldwyn-Mayer had Leo the Lion with his mighty roar, we had Blue giving a true bark.

That clip of her barking was filmed at the end of a photo shoot that *Sports Illustrated* did with Dad in the Bruins dressing room. In fact, you can see one of the millions they took on the cover of *Grapes: A Vintage View of Hockey*. It's hard to believe he had a daughter who groomed dogs when you look at the length of Blue's nails in that picture. The photographers had a lot of lights and they kept popping. All you have to do is look into those evil blue eyes to see that Blue was not a happy camper. When they filmed her barking it was a true half growl, half bark. That experience ruined getting a nice picture of her for the rest of her life. Speaking of her bark, I never liked the one they dubbed in for her in the opening of Coach's Corner. It sounded so wimpy.

It was indeed a show to be proud of, especially in the array of guests Dad interviewed. Not only did the hockey greats come on, like Jean Beliveau, Rocket Richard, Wayne Gretzky, and Scotty Bowman, to name a few, but also Joe Frazier, Ron Luciano, Ben Johnson, and sportscasters Danny Gallivan, Dick Beddoes, and Dick Irvin, Jr. Dad did two and sometimes three shows a night—not bad for a shoestring budget. But that was Gerry: he said he would make it happen and he did.

It was about this time that things became a bit strained between Gerry and Dad, mostly due to the quick expansion of the restaurant businesses. Gerry's other business ventures outside of Dad's were having a tough time. Of course, Dad blamed this on Gerry's trusting nature. Dad, on the other hand, was street-smart. He didn't have blinders on when it came to good talkers and figured people out quickly. I was always amazed when we'd leave a business meeting and I'd say, "What do you think?" If he said, "No good," that was the end of it. But sometimes what some people would deem a put-down he'd mean as a compliment, such as when he'd call a person a "shark," there would be nothing wrong with that. Sharks are cunning and survivalist. One time he said, "He reminds me of an American." Now to some, especially Canadians, that would be a negative, but I knew it was a compliment. When he called someone a "wise old owl," most would think it was a compliment, but it wasn't. It's best described as "mansplaining" but for both genders. I used this term to describe a new board member on Rose Cherry's Home for Kids to our chairperson. He said, "I'm glad you liked her." I then had to explain to him that her long, drawn-out explanations were due to her thinking we were too stupid to follow her thought process. This was just before I left the board.

I love using metaphors for describing people. One time Dad asked me what I thought of an individual we had a business luncheon with who was pitching an idea. I said he reminded me of a Ferengi in *Star Trek*, a kind of scheming, goblin-like alien species. Unfortunately Dad had never watched *Star Trek*, but Tim knew exactly what I meant and agreed, and therefore Dad passed on this new business venture.

As time went on, stress made its way to Gerry in the form of Bell's palsy. To some degree I believe his family blamed it on Dad. Dad's career was taking off and Gerry's boxes were all coming true, and somehow they felt Gerry was being left behind. This might have been true to a minor degree, especially concerning the restaurants. Sure, Dad had a separate business partner for them, but Gerry also had business partners apart from the endeavours with Dad. They didn't go their separate ways, but life evolved.

Soon after the TV and radio shows, plus the franchises, came the *Rock'em Sock'em* tapes. I say "tapes," but let's face it, they evolved too, from VHS to DVD to Blue-ray and collection series. When they started in

1989, Mom came up with the name. It was pretty catchy until Mattel, the manufacturer of Rock 'Em Sock 'Em Robots, came calling. From 1998–2007 (volumes 11–19) Dad's tapes are called "Don Cherry's Hockey." This was when the name dispute was settled, and it returned to its original name.

These tapes were staples as stocking stuffers at Christmas for many hockey families. Lots of hockey moms used to say to Dad, "I keep the kids busy on Christmas day while I am cooking by playing your tape." Some NHL players even mentioned them on TV when being interviewed about a great goal or save: "Maybe it will make it on *Rock'em Sock'em*." NHL greats loved these tapes, like Jason Spezza, who said, "A large part of my youth was spent watching *Rock'em Sock'em*. It's right in my wheelhouse. We'd get one tape for Christmas and watch it all year, over and over. They're iconic." Maybe that was why he was Dad's Mississauga IceDog's number-one pick in the OHL priority draft in 1999.

Hall of Famer Mark Messier was quoted in *The Hockey News* saying, "I, like any other Canadian, would watch the highlights. At the time we didn't have the media when it first started and the accessibility to see what was going on in the league. So when these videos came out, it really took the country by storm. It was a big part of our game."

Swedish-born defenseman Niklas Kronwall, a triple gold-club member (winning a gold medal in both the Olympics and World Championships, plus a Stanley Cup with the Red Wings), said that watching the videos helped Europeans learn the game.

Left winger Taylor Hall fondly said, "Probably my biggest memory would be when I was in junior; the *Rock'em Sock'em* would find its way on the DVD or the TV quite often. I can remember seeing the same one more than once."

Many times, if a player had a good fight or goal, they'd say to Dad, "Hope that makes it on your tape."

If you were a collector of these tapes, it was interesting to see how Tim and Dad would change it up every year, from the content to the locations. For instance, volume 7 had segments filmed at the Hockey Hall of Fame in Toronto. Number 29 was filmed in Kingston at the International Hockey Hall of Fame, now known as the "Original Hockey Hall of Fame," which was close to Dad's heart. For years he tried to get it into a new prime location in the heart of downtown Kingston on Tragically Hip Way, which was right around the corner from where the Major Junior A Frontenacs played. Though this sounds like it makes a lot of sense, the politicians of Kingston voted against it and put it way out in the suburbs in a community centre. So, to give it some type of notoriety, he filmed a segment there. Plus, they filmed at the Hershey Centre in Mississauga for volume 11 in 1999, titled *The New Millennium*, which has my favourite bloopers at the end. Other locations were where the Hurricanes practiced at Rexall Place in Edmonton during the 2006 Stanley Cup finals; the Prudential Center in New Jersey, where the Kings practiced during their Stanley Cup run; the Spectrum in Philadelphia, home of the Flyers; and let us not forget the old Maple Leaf Gardens, now known as the Mattamy Athletic Centre.

I have several fond memories of these tapes. One is the fun we had at our Peter Street (now known as Blue Jay Way) bar where we filmed volume 5. There was a pool table there, and Dad (who's an excellent billiards player) wanted to do a bank shot and then cut to the video to show players doing it with the puck against the boards. They filmed a few times, as Dad was determined to make the shot and not rely on editing, as most pool scenes in movies do. However, he also wanted Blue watching with her front legs on the table. This was a challenge, because she didn't feel comfortable standing on the chair as they were filming. My poor mother was on the floor trying to steady Blue to get the shot. You can see her frustration in the bloopers at the end of the tape.

Another favourite was three-year-old Del's debut sitting on his grandfather's lap in our basement. This segment had Dad lecturing parents about kids' hockey by advising them on their equipment, when to start, etc. I can never understand parents putting their kids in skates and then right onto slippery ice. They can hardly walk while trying to balance themselves on the thin blades, let alone doing it on ice. And they wonder why so many give up skating. As soon as Del learned to walk he was in skates with layers of tape on the blades, and that's how he walked around the house. He got so good at keeping his balance that I took the laces out so he would have to balance even more. It's hard to believe that eighteen years later he would become the associate producer, in volume 25.

Next to the bloopers at the end of each tape, I enjoyed the musical interludes. First seen in volume 2, "Grape Jam" was introduced. It had a lot of great clips of Dad as a player, coaching, and on Coach's Corner. Of course there were scenes of fights, brawls, players turtling, and refs he didn't like, all set to a catchy beat. The lyrics, addressing visors, European players, and fighting in hockey, would be questionable today. All this was jammed (excuse the pun) in a minute and a half.

A radio DJ named Chris Shepard, along with Hennie Bekker and Greg Kavanaugh, formed a Canadian techno group called BKS and developed Rock'em Sock'em Techno for volume 5. This video had Dad dancing in his long red leather coat in a fedora and sunglasses. It had everything in it, including DJ Chris spinning the records, lots of smoke, and girls dancing to the beat, along with hockey hits, goals, saves, and, of course, fights. It was a very entertaining two and half minutes, even though MuchMusic voted it the worst video of 1993, in spite of its popularity.

These tapes didn't come without their critics. Dad addressed them by saying, "It's pretty funny when the left-wingers criticize everything I do and they say Don Cherry's *Rock'em Sock'em*s are full of fights, but they would have to watch it to know that we have two or three fights in a minute and a half [of the entire video]. It's absolutely ridiculous, because kids are watching the fights during the hockey game."

You also have to know that the NHL approved every bit of footage. And yes, the fights they chose to show were evenly matched bouts in which neither player badly pummels the other. Plus, they limited the showing of career-ending hits such as Matt Cooke's on Marc Savard. One humorous objection was to a reference in the commentary to Philadelphia's Broad Street Bullies. No matter how it was explained to them that this was a known nickname to the Flyers, not Don Cherry calling them bullies, it was deemed unacceptable.

As with all good things, like the radio and TV show, Dad knew *Rock'em Sock'em* had run its course after thirty years. With technology and distribution rights constantly changing, Dad and Tim knew they were wrapping it up at just the right time. It had become Canada's all-time best-selling non-theatrical DVD collection. That is something to be proud of.

Also included within Gerry's TV boxes was appearances on HNiC. In the beginning Dad would do colour with the play-by-play announcer. It wasn't until they developed a segment called Coach's Corner that things turned around. I can remember my mother saying, "Well, it's only going to be five to seven minutes long—how much trouble can he get in within that short period of time?" Little did she know.

Dad started bucking the system of HNiC right off the bat by not wanting to wear their standard baby blue jackets. The HNiC crew was noted for wearing them, but Dad would have none of it. Thank goodness that the executive producer, Ralph Mellanby, who also produced the Grapevine show, knew how to handle situations like this. In the beginning, another crisis was that CBC wanted him to go to a course on how to "enunciate his words better." Poor Ralph used to joke that there are two official languages in Canada, and Don doesn't speak either. He certainly was a good friend to Dad, and a master at his craft. He won five Emmy Awards, produced both Winter and Summer Olympics, covered both the CFL and MLB, and was an author. I could go on and on. However, his most significant achievement to me was the development of Coach's Corner and, as he used to say, "inflicting Don Cherry on the unassuming Canadian audience."

Gerry saw Dad as an author within his boxes from the beginning. He convinced Mom and Dad they had a story that needed to be written. Gerry is mentioned in the acknowledgments of *Grapes, A Vintage View of Hockey*. It was agreed that hockey historian Stan Fischler would assist Dad in his newest endeavour. When I read it, even I, knowing and living most of the stories, was captivated by the style of Dad's writing. It's an easy-to-read book, more about life than sports; however, writing it did have its challenges for both Mom and Dad.

Dad wrote by hand and talked into a mini tape recorder in telling his story for the book. He'd send the notes and tapes off to Stan, who'd translate it into "proper" English, using up-to-date terminology to describe hockey. For instance, what Dad referred to as "our end" and "their end" are now called the "offensive and defensive zones." What Dad would term the "middle of the ice" is now referenced as the "neutral zone." When Dad received his revisions, he would blow a gasket. It sounded nothing like him, and he wanted it to be read like he talked. This means short sentences and getting to the point fast. When he saw that they used terms not even used in hockey, like "dribbling the puck," it set him off. There would be rewrite after rewrite, but he would not get worn down until he got his way.

Finally the publisher and Stan figured out that he was not going to cave, and this book was going to be in his style, not someone else's. Because of this process the book took a while to write, all while they were living at the cottage. It got to a point where Mom would hide the mail and not show him the rewritten chapters until after dinner. When you read the first book, know that it was made with a lot of love, hate, and other emotions. There is a picture on the back flap of Dad grabbing Stan Fischler, with a caption saying, "Don explaining the McEwen incident to Stan." Who knows, maybe he was thinking of all the rewrites he had to do!

After it was published, women would come up to me and say how much they enjoyed it. This was strange, because we considered it a sports book that men would read, not women. They explained that it was more about life than hockey. Men told me it was the first time they had seen their wives reading a sports book in bed and giggling. These are the tests for a book: whether you can immerse yourself in it, and if it appeals to all. You didn't have to know hockey to relate to what Dad went through in his life. Most of it was non-identifiable to the reader, which made it more entertaining. It reminds me of how many women approached me about *Keep Your Head Up, Kid*. Moms would say it was the first sports movie the whole family could enjoy together. It was a love story for the moms, with a hockey aspect for the kids and dads. You had the feel of what hockey is really like, with no swearing, a feat that is tough to do. One man told me he watched it with his elderly mother and was given quite a scolding afterwards. Her son hadn't told her that the woman his mom so admired in the movie dies at the end. He said, "My mother doesn't cry over any movies, but she sure did over yours."

If you read the epilogue in *Grapes, A Vintage View of Hockey*, you get the feeling that it was his first and last book. I think he had no ambition or foresight to write another one. Little did he know that there would be five more. As he said to Mom about the radio shows: who knew he had that many stories in him? I personally love his style of writing and how he talks. That's the beauty of it. You can hear him telling the story. There is no ego in it, for he repeatedly talks about the life lessons he learned, or should have, plus constantly questioning himself why he does the things he does. He doesn't justify anything and lets you be the judge of him. He tries to convince you of nothing.

Gerry's gone now. He died of a heart attack helping someone shovel their driveway. I knew his funeral would be spectacular, for his widow, Trudy, who worked at *Chatelaine Magazine*'s food department, would put on an amazing spread. What happened at the funeral was at first horrifying, then deemed acceptable. She had a pamphlet printed for the evening. Somehow Dad ended up standing beside her at the casket for the receiving line. People were giving their condolences to her, and some person in line, brandishing their pamphlet, asked Dad for his autograph on "this program." He always has a Sharpie in his jacket and obliged, with Trudy nodding and smiling in what seemed to be her approval. I was watching from way back and was aghast. My mother, God rest her soul, would have been horrified. But somehow Trudy was smiling and didn't seem to mind. She would ask the people to whom they would like it signed and how to spell their names. Once one person started, it was the thing to do. I don't know how God took it, but I knew Gerry was up in heaven laughing himself silly. Afterwards, I mentioned to Dad, "Well, that was certainly a first." He asked what else he was supposed to do. Trudy seemed all right with it and was encouraging, so he kept going. She too knew it was something Gerry would have loved.

Throughout the years, all of Gerry's boxes came to fruition: the speaking engagements, radio and TV shows, a chain of restaurants, six book deals, and a thirty-year run on DVDs, plus owning a Major Junior A team. Throughout all this came endorsements, voiceovers, and, yes, even a bit of acting. Was this all planned, as in Gerry's boxes? Perhaps Dad had a vision, but he and Mom could never have imagined it all. I would say it evolved. People would often ask me, "Who is Don's agent? Does he really have one?" Perhaps he had people or acquaintances who brought him opportunities, but when it came down to decisions it was Mom and Dad telling marketing and advertising people what he would and would not do. Dad would have no problem if he didn't get his way in something, such as saying a particular line. He'd have no problem just saying, "Fine. The deal is off." I believe that, in every contract he ever signed, the last line in fine print would be, "Don has final approval." People don't realize that money, although a motivator, didn't dictate Mom's and Dad's lives. They were quite happy in Mississauga. Dad had an income from HNiC, so the rest was just gravy.

CHAPTER 17

IN BETWEEN LIFE

Some may wonder what Don Cherry does in his spare time. Let's face it, he worked seven minutes per week in the winter. Most people have hobbies to relax, but trust me, he has none. His vacations are limited to the cottage. If you'd like to generalize what he does in his spare time, it's reading and watch TV. He does odd jobs or projects around the house, usually involving cleaning. He's either tidying the car, shed, garage, or aquarium, filling up bird feeders, or organizing his office.

If he does go out, his favourite thing is scouting for the Ontario Hockey League with Tim. This all came to an abrupt end when the pandemic hit in 2020. Tim was a part of the OHL's central scouting, rating players in the greater Toronto and Hamilton area. He would watch the games of players who were fifteen, in a section of the Greater Toronto Hockey League (GTHL) that used to be called Triple A Minor Midget but for obvious reasons is now called the Under 16 Division. These were the kids who would be drafted into the OHL the following season. My brother could give recommendations to parents on how to act in the presence of scouts. One time when I was with them a mother was yelling to the point of being annoying, which is rare among Triple A parents. The question among the scouts would be, *Whose mother is she?* It would be noted that this mother was troubled, and this might affect the kid's chances. Watching parents of Triple A kids is a lot different than watching the Double A's. There is not much shouting or even clapping with Triple A. The parents have been around the block and know what is at stake. Sometimes I couldn't even tell if they had scored, for there was never much fanfare compared to the lower ranks.

Tim has endless stories about the dynamics of it all when he was out with Dad. One time they drove to Welland, Ontario, which is over an hour's drive from their home. They wanted to see a kid by the name of James Tardif, who played Provincial Junior A on the Cougars. About 30 seconds into the game, doesn't he get thrown out? There were a lot of other scouts there, and within a couple of minutes the rink was about empty except for parents. Now, what do Tim and Dad do? They knew it was starting to snow and truly wanted to leave like everyone else, but no. Dad didn't want to hurt all the other players' feelings, so they stayed for the whole game. James came up to them to say hello, and Dad gave him a pizza he had won in the game raffle. It was always amusing how often Dad would win either the 50/50 draws or the pizzas. He would always donate it back. A couple of weeks later, Dad got a lovely letter from the opposing coach of that game telling him how much it meant to the players that he had stayed and watched them play till the end. It's people like that, who know the culture of hockey, that would recognize a gesture like Dad had made. Another instance like this was when they were at a Junior D Uxbridge Bruins' game, the last one on a Friday night, and doesn't it go into triple overtime? Dad and Tim hung in there till about two a.m., then had to leave knowing that Ron would be calling him in about four hours to discuss Coach's Corner. Even then they got razzed about leaving, when some of the fathers said they too had get up earlier the next day, some to milk cows. Hopefully they appreciated Dad and Tim's effort in staying that long.

Tim used to come to some of my son's Double A games. He still talks about a mom on our team who always brought an annoying cowbell. He couldn't get over how she clanged it when a kid on the other team really got nailed. Even Dad commented on this woman's choice of what she cheered for. But if you had a kid in minor hockey, you couldn't say anything or you'd quickly get labelled a troublemaker. My time as a hockey mom truly tested my patience with other people. If there was ever a case of someone dummying themselves down, it would be me in my era of dealing with minor hockey.

It was a real treat sitting with some of the parents whose kids are now playing in the NHL and hearing the real gossip. They would comment about what they called the "black crows." I asked whom they were referring to, and it was the scouts. They were all known for wearing black jackets, sitting or standing way up high in the stands and commenting on and judging their kids. I often wondered if this was a reference to the crows in Disney's 1941 version of *Dumbo*.

Tim scouted for about fifteen years, and would go out from two to four nights a week. Dad would often go with him, for he enjoyed watching the kids play. If you ask me, it was because it reminded him not only of playing minor hockey, but playing pro. Dad played for very little money, mostly for the love of the game. You could see that these kids also played for the love of the game, but they didn't have wives and kids to support!

That is why, if you are a true hockey fan and want to watch a fast-paced, entertaining form of hockey, you should go to an Under 16 game in the GTHL. I used to go out with them every now and then, for the games were very exciting. The players were skilled and the games always had a good pace. It is here that one could see future NHL stars develop, such as Connor McDavid, Max Domi, John Tavares, Mitchell Marner, Darnell Nurse, Ryan O'Reilly, Tyler Seguin, Shane Wright, and many more. It's amazing that this one Canadian minor league produced seventy-eight players who played in the 2022–23 NHL season.

Two of the biggest rivalries in the GTHL are the Don Mills Flyers and the Toronto Marlies. These two teams meet often in their regular schedule and many times in the OHL Cup. One of the most exciting games in its history was when the Marlies were down by three goals and came back to score five in the third period. The game-winner went in with twenty seconds left in the game, and they then scored on an open net. When these two teams got together it was always exciting. In fact, the last fight Dad and Tim saw when scouting was a line brawl between these two. Everyone squared off, including Max Domi against a much larger player, and they took their helmets off. They were throwing punches and slowly drifting towards the boards, ending up right in front of where Max's Dad, Tie, was standing. Everyone was thinking the same thing: *Please, Lord, don't let this kid clock Max.* All were afraid of what Tie might do. Tim told me that, while all the dads were watching the action on the ice, all the moms were staring daggers at Dad, for somehow it was his fault.

When you scout with Dad and Tim and your kid plays minor hockey, you get to know the quirks of each rink: which has the best parking, popcorn, hot chocolate, dressing rooms, and, most of all, which is the coldest.

One of the chilliest is the community rinks at the Hershey Centre. Del used to play there, and I would dread it. Some rinks have an option for you to watch in a warmer area, instead of the freezing cold. If you stayed where it was warm, I felt you weren't into your kid's hockey game. However, this philosophy changed if there was an option to sit in a bar or restaurant and have a drink or two while watching.

I liked going out with them for the 9:30 weeknight games, as the referees would want to get the game over quickly. Let's face it, the kids had school the next day and these refs had to get up for work the next morning. Because of this they'd just let them play the game. There were no chintzy penalties called and the kids knew it. This makes a difference in ways you may not think of. A non-hockey person might presume, *Oh, now the kids will play dirty because they think they can get away with it.* This is not the case at all; in fact, it's the opposite. If the ref starts calling a lot of cheap penalties, the players' mindsets change and the game gets rougher and meaner. The kids' logic is, *If I am going to get a penalty for doing practically nothing, then I will make it a good one.* This is when the referees lose control of the game, and it's bedlam.

At one of these games the ref was doing a great job, but called a chintzy penalty on the team that was losing late in the third period. I asked Tim what that was all about and he pointed to the scoreboard, which showed 3–0, and his watch. I remembered that if there is a four-goal differential the clock will go to straight time, which is when the clock keeps running even during stoppages of play. It's then that the coaches take a long time changing shifts, and the refs are in no hurry to line the kids up for the faceoff—anything to run down the clock so everyone can go home.

Dad and Tim liked to sit by themselves. When I went with them, it was very quiet. Tim and Dad didn't talk much during the game, they just watched and made a few comments here and there. The one thing that drove Dad nuts was when people nearby were talking during the game.

He didn't mind if they were cheering their team on, but countless times people would be sitting near Dad, talking about the vacation they were not going on because their son was playing hockey.

The worst was when they were alone and two guys would sit nearby and start talking loudly to impress Dad with their hockey knowledge. They'd begin to say stupid stuff, like what some kid should have done, or what the Leafs need to do. Dad would stare daggers at them, and then Tim and Dad would move.

When a scout or parent sat near them and they didn't take their eyes off their phone, Dad took notice. He mentioned that either the parent didn't care about their kid's game or the scout wasn't doing his job. It was amazing that he saw any of the game while he stared at them.

One of their favourite places to stand was at the Zamboni door in rink 1 at Etobicoke Ice Sports. Del has played there many times and I can tell you that it is one of the coldest rinks in the Toronto area. Tim and Dad would stand by the Zamboni door when they flooded the rink, for it was pretty warm there. I often wondered why this was so, and Tim finally explained it to me: unlike other rinks that dump the scraped ice from the Zamboni outside, they would dump it in a huge cement pit inside. Above this pit were heaters to melt the ice. They didn't want to waste valuable parking spaces.

In this same area was a huge hot water heater with a large insulation wrap. The insulation was white and one day Dad started to sign it, as he always had his Sharpie with him. He'd write something like "Don Cherry, Jan 3/2012, watching Connor McDavid and Marlies." Or he'd write something about the Marlies' Christmas tournament (now called the Holiday Classic Tournament). It started in 1931, and it's a major showpiece of minor league talent. That is why over 200 OHL, OHA, and U.S. college scouts attend it. Dad wrote on this water heater for many years—even Ron wrote on it. This thing read like a time capsule of hockey but it's long gone, and I wonder if anyone got a kick out of reading it like I did.

One time Ron came out with Dad and Tim to watch a game. They were standing along the ice in a corner near the dressing room doors. Late in the period there was a big hit right in front of one of the benches. One of the players went down on the ice and there was a lot of blood. The player lost a few teeth, even with a cage and a mouthguard. He went to the dressing room, and suddenly the mother came storming down furious, staring daggers at Dad and Ron as if it were their fault. Ron made a comment but she didn't say a word. If looks could kill they both would have been dead. When the period was over, there was a delay in cleaning the ice. Dad and Ron asked the trainer, "Did he find his tooth?" They hadn't, but the trainer said they could put it back in if they found it, so Ron, Dad, and the trainer went out on the ice to look for it. Ron even got down on his knees to look, to no avail. Then the Zamboni started beeping its horn for them to get off the ice. I think Dad would have liked to present the tooth to the mom.

Dad loved seeing the young players wearing shirts and ties into the rinks. It showed respect for the game, and many kids were proud to wear them. When they would come up for a selfie, Dad always commented on how good they looked in their shirts and ties. How many places can a ten-year-old gets dressed up for? This transitioned to Coach's Corner, when he'd show clips of NHLers walking into the rinks. He'd show a winning team dressed up versus a losing team that had relaxed their dress code.

Going to tournaments was tougher on Dad because many of these teams had never seen him in the rinks before. As with all tournaments, it was a constant flow of players coming and going. At this tournament, a team came up to take a photo wearing tracksuits. When they were finished, the next team came up, all wearing shirts and ties. Dad asked the kids, "Why didn't that last team look as sharp as you guys?" With disdain, one of the kids said, "They're Americans."

It was a different reception for Dad and Tim's first venture out for scouting after Poppygate. Though these were "his" people, instead of "those" people who took offence to his reference, they didn't know how to approach Dad now. I guess they wondered if he was still as receptive to people coming up to him as before. Of course, it took a hockey mom to break the ice. She had brought cupcakes to the game to celebrate her son's birthday and offered Dad one, which he graciously accepted. She asked if he'd take a picture with her son holding the cupcake. Her son was embarrassed by the whole thing, but that's what mothers do, and I am sure that picture will be valued in years to come. Once everyone saw that it was the same old Don, approachable, receptive, and friendly, it was game on. One by one everyone came up and told him their interpretation of that infamous broadcast. The one common denominator was that they would spew venom toward Ron. To hear such passion in their voices sure meant a lot to us, especially after getting bashed in the press the way Dad had been. It was as if they had to let off steam because they couldn't say it anywhere else. We never added fuel to the fire, just thanked them for their kind words.

Many people would be surprised at what Dad values. For instance, he is an avid collector of Royal Doulton, particularly the Toby mugs and the Balloon Lady series. This goes back to when he bought his mother a Balloon Lady figurine in the sixties. Sadly, when she was out of town a neighbour called Dad up to tell him her house had been broken into and, believe it or not, they had stolen the Balloon Lady. What sophisticated thieves they have in Kingston. Dad had it replaced before she got home. I can distinctly remember both pieces. The original one was so detailed you could see the veins in her hands and the wrinkles in her face and clothes. The new one was very disappointing in that everything was smooth. My grandmother knew it was a replacement but never let on. It's sad to see the quality go down from a company that has been around since 1815. Dad gave me his white and tan Bulldog statue that he has had since 1955. It is very detailed, showing the muscles and wrinkles of the dog, compared to the collectable Jack the Bulldog seen in the James Bond movie *No Time to Die*. I treasure it and is on my mantel.

Years ago, a friend's grandmother passed and I went over to give her my condolences. She mentioned that Dad had gone to the hospital to see her grandmother—I didn't even know he knew her. He brought her a Royal Doulton piece, one of the many ladies they feature. She told me how her grandmother cherished it and gave it to her when she died. I told her to look underneath it, as Dad always writes something on things he gives away. Sure enough, he had written her name and the date he had visited her. My friend never knew it was there. Dad once gave me the Country Rose figurine. I got up from the computer while writing this and looked under it too: "Given to Cindy Cherry for her great work on Rose Cherry Home for Kids, Woodbine Races made $45,000. Oct 3, '04." I, like my friend, never knew it was there until now.

He does enjoy watching TV, but it's usually baseball or hockey, the History Channel and Turner Classic Movies. His expertise in history is astounding. You'd never believe he quit school after the ninth grade. He is an avid reader, with a vast range of knowledge. This may have come from his father, who read Horatio Alger's bedtime stories to him when he was young. He still has several of those books. The stories all have the same plot of an impoverished boy rising from a humble background to become successful. They are rags-to-riches stories with the belief that hard work, honesty, and determination can conquer all. This scenario sounds familiar.

One of his favourite subjects to read about is the Antarctic explorer Robert Falcon Scott, otherwise known as Scott of the Antarctic. Scott wanted to be the first person to reach the South Pole. He died on the journey. I asked why he liked this topic so much, and Dad said he liked when Scott, in his tent and knowing he was going to die, wrote in his diary, and even took the time to dot his i's and cross his t's. Maybe that's why Dad is big on autographs being readable. I apply this rule every day of my life. Whether I am writing Christmas, birthday or thank-you cards, or just signing my name, I will always go back and check to see if all my i's and t's are dotted and crossed. I figure if Robert Scott can do it, how lazy would I be not to?

One Christmas I wanted to get Dad a book on Roald Amundsen, the Norwegian Antarctic explorer who beat Scott to the South Pole and made it back alive. The book was rather expensive, so I checked to make sure this was a book he'd want to read. To my surprise, he said he would not read any books on Amundsen. When I asked why, he said that to survive this trip back from the South Pole, Amundsen ate some of his sled dogs. As far as Dad was concerned, that was not honourable.

Other favourite subjects of Dad's are Lord Admiral Horatio Nelson, Sir Francis Drake, T. E. Lawrence (a.k.a. Lawrence of Arabia), Ernest Shackleton, and Sir Francis Chichester, and biographies of old-time movie stars. Dad also has an extensive collection of antique books on Arctic and Antarctic exploration and British naval history. One of the main places Tim would buy such books is an antique bookshop in Toronto called David Mason Books.

After a while, Dad wanted to go to this bookstore and browse. Well, Dad doesn't casually browse, so we knew he would buy a ton of books.

While at the bookstore he met David Mason and his wife, Deb. David is right out of central casting as an owner of a store that sells antique and rare books, and they hit it off instantly. After a short talk about the Leafs, Dad and David started to talk about books, authors, and some of Dad's heroes. It got to the point that David would put some books aside for Dad during the year so Tim could pick them up when he stopped by.

David told Dad a funny story. Some of the circles David runs in are the academic and book worlds. The academic world is not a place where Dad is in good standing. While at parties within these circles, sometimes Dad's name would come up and they'd trash him in front of David. After they were finished, David would ask, "Have you ever met Don Cherry?" They would all say no. David would go on to say how he and Don were friends, which is accurate, and how Dad has an extensive collection of antique books. He would tell them how they'd have long conversations about T. E. Lawrence and his book *Seven Pillars of Wisdom*, among other things. David said that would shut them up quickly, and the topic of the discussion would change. So if you're ever looking for an antique book, check out David Mason Books in Toronto.

Many people who don't like Dad have difficulty believing that he is interested and well-read on many topics outside of hockey. When the Royal Ontario Museum had an exhibit on the city of Pompeii, Dad wanted to see it. Not that Dad would complain, but at times going out in public becomes an autograph session. So Tim called the ROM, said that Dad wanted to see the exhibit, and asked for a good time to visit to avoid the crowds. They were very helpful and told Tim and Dad to go down on a particular day and time. A museum curator met Dad and took him on a tour of the exhibit. Dad and Tim were wandering around the rest of the museum after they were through looking at the Pompeii exhibit when an older guard noticed Dad and Tim looking at a statue. He approached them and said, "Are you Don Cherry?" Dad responded in his usual comeback to this all too familiar question: "It's either another good-looking guy or me." The guard gave Dad an up-and-down look and said, "You don't look like a museum guy to me." Dad said, "What does a museum guy look like?" "Not you," the guard replied. Dad and Tim laughed it off.

I think this curator reflects many people's opinions about Dad, whether good or bad. Society likes to categorize people, especially when we pay attention to social media, which can put a spin on just about anything to get its views across. There are even people going for university degrees by analyzing Don Cherry. One soon-to-be graduate titled theirs, "Don Cherry's Final Rant: Illuminating Canadian Nationalism, Racial Xenophobia [is there any other kind?] and Hegemonic Masculinity." One of these highly educated students studied Coach's Corner for their dissertation research while examining "the intersection of gender and Canadian national identity within the sport of men's ice hockey."

I guess Dad should take all these academics analyzing him as a form of flattery. I've read some of the published articles, and they are way off-target. Even though they're wrong, it's amazing that one man giving his opinion for seven minutes a week for nine months out of the year evokes such passion. Don't you think?

1972 Playoff Champions

PITTSFORD HIGH SCHOOL

1971 - 72 Monroe County High School

League - Regular Season Champions

16 Wins   0 Losses   0 Ties

First team that Dad cut his teeth regarding the art
of coaching. Check out their record

Teammate Floyd Smith with his wife Audrey giving me my first teddy bear. They played 4 years together on Eddie Shore's Springfield Indians

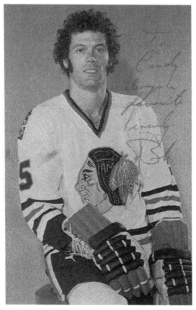

Bob Kelly, dad's first enforcer that I knew that taped his knuckles

Dad's stylish 1972/73 Rochester Amerks: Lft to Rt-Dave Hrechkosy, Gene Sobchuck, John Bednarski, ?, & Battleship Kelly

Tim & I didn't go on the cruise, just as well, as Dad & Mom flew home.

Ever the entrepreneurs, Mom & Dad's Rochester Hockey School.
Note: Dick Mattiussi (far rt standing, replaced Dad as coach
of the Amerks, when he went on to coach the Bruins.

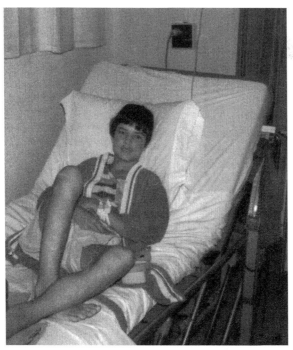

Tim in his private room at the Mass General Hospital

Me & all my flowers at the hospital getting prepped for our kidney transplant

Kingston's hockey cowboys: Dad, his brother Richard & Wayne
Cashman who played together in 1970/71 on the Oklahoma
City Blazers of the CHL (Central Hockey League)

At my 60th surprise party, with Tim & that kidney
still going strong. Got to be a record by now!

My first car! Love those huge powerful Monte Carlos

Darryl Sittler with Dad, Sept. 15, 1976, after he scored the overtime
goal against the Czechs to win the inaugural Canada Cup.

Cdn Cup celebrations, with (lft to rt) Lanny McDonald,
Carol Vadnais, Coach Cherry, Bob Gainey

Gerry Patterson who owned S.E.T. Production Co., that developed This Week in Hockey & The Grapevine Show, along with its producer, Tim Cherry and the star of the show

Lft to Rt-Scott Stevens, Dad, Jimmy Loftus & Steve Yzerman @ a Grapevine Show taping

Good Kingston Boy, Kirk Muller. Dad wore sunglasses as we
thought he had poison ivy, but years later we figured it was really
Shingles, from all the stress he was under taping the TV show

Rocket Maurice Richard who played 18 seasons with the Canadians,
winning 8 Stanley Cups & had 14 All-Star appearances

Wayne Gretzky, who graciously invited Mom & Dad to his 1988 wedding to Janet Jones. Dad then proceeded to keep the invite as a memento, but later forgot what book he put it in for safekeeping, never to be seen again.

Joe Frazier, who changed the flat tire on the limo that was driving him to a taping of the Grapevine show at our bar in Hamilton

Dick Irvin (rt) HNIC broadcaster from 1976-1999, with Red
Storey who played & officiated in football, lacrosse & hockey.

Tim, the producer of Canada's all-time best selling non-
theatrical collection of DVD's, numbering at 30

Long-time friends of the Cherry Family, Mel & Bev Price, with Dad &
Mark Potter, at the Original Hockey Hall of Fame, formerly known as
the International HH of Fame, located in the Invista Centre, Kingston.

Dad & grandson Del; Why he has a
Flames sweater on, I have no idea

EPILOGUE

So, how has Dad rebounded after Poppygate? Remember, the pandemic hit soon afterwards, affecting everyone's lifestyle. It tested many people's resilience to change and adaptability. Can you imagine the role that Coach's Corner played in his life for thirty-seven years? And then boom, it was gone. He took the slings and arrows and stayed true to himself, and that is all his fans and family would ask of him.

However, we believed many people still wanted to hear Dad's opinions about hockey and other topics the CBC were forever trying to muzzle him about. My brother didn't miss a beat in putting together Don Cherry's Grapevine Podcast.

Del, Tim, Dad & me, celebrating our
podcast success; Christmas 2020

In 2020, Apple Podcasts voted it "Best of the Year," and it has been listened to by over 4 million people worldwide. I have to give credit where credit is due when addressing whether we were "worthy" of attracting a sponsor for the podcast. The hesitation that companies had in initially sponsoring the podcast, shows how corporations were leery of associating themselves with Don Cherry. However, one that did step up to the plate with no fear of public resistance was spreads.ca. (Now known as NorthStar Bets).

Proving Spreads.ca/NorthStar Bets
support for animal rescue

They have been very generous to Don Cherry's Pet Rescue Foundation by raising funds and donating over $24,000 throughout the years. It makes you wonder, with all the choices of gambling sites out there, why it wouldn't be a no-brainer for Canadians to choose this one for their betting needs. They're Canadian-owned, cover all major North American and international sports, have an impressive casino game collection, use Canadian money, and give back to pet rescue—what's not to love?

It's a family affair, with my dad and brother talking not only about hockey, but personal stuff too. I sit in and give my two cents, but I limit my input, though I feel I have much more to say. I took my cue off a guy who informed me that he wished I'd stop interrupting Dad and let him finish a sentence. Ouch! I'll admit, I could give my opinion a lot more on that podcast, but believe it or not, Dad has to hold me back so I don't hurt anyone's feelings. This came after I gave my opinion on Carey Price and his situation with the Montreal Canadiens. If you haven't come to your own conclusion after reading this book, Dad is a lot kinder than I am on many topics.

Signatures of people who assist the producer. Grace is Tim's daughter (photographer) & Ling is his wife providing Craft service. Note my contribution: filler

We get together every Sunday morning, have coffee, get caught up on our week, then record the podcast on Tim's dining room table. After we're finished, Tim's wife makes a wonderful lunch. It's great family time and I cherish it so. ------------

In closing, I think a clip from 2008 on the Rick Mercer Show sums up everything. In it, Rick asks Dad, "Do you worry sometimes that you are going to go on television, it's live, you don't have anyone in your ear, you're going to say something and then you'll going to go down in a ball of flames?" Dad replies, "everyone expects it". Rick confirms, "If you ask people how is Cherry going to go out, it's in a ball of flames," as Dad replies, "or a trainwreck."

To this, I add, Ron asked Dad if he did it all on purpose. I told him Tim and I wondered the same thing. In our eyes, you couldn't have written a better exit plan. He denies it, but I'll always wonder.

EPILOGUE PART 2

Growing up, Cindy and I quickly learned that holidays and birthdays were celebrated when the hockey schedule allowed. When Dad played in the AHL, he often played on Christmas and New Year's Day. So Christmas Dinner was on Christmas Eve or Boxing Day. Same with birthdays. Cindy's birthday is in March, so most of the time, Dad played or coached on her birthday. Mom's birthday was in December, and Dad's was in February. If Dad was on the road, we waited until he got home. As a family we rarely had a big dinner together and usually never on the holiday date.

After Poppygate, we started our podcast. We would record it Sunday morning in my kitchen, and then my wife would make a big lunch. So it became a family tradition to have a Sunday lunch with Del, my daughter Grace, my wife, Dad, and Cindy. During the playoffs, Dad would come over to my house to watch the game, and Cindy would usually drop by after she was done working. Looking back, little did Dad and I know how precious those days were.

All that would change on July 15th, 2024. My sister, who donated her kidney to me so I could live a normal life, suddenly passed away. Our lives have changed forever, and our Sunday lunches don't seem the same.

Tim Cherry, Cindy's always grateful brother.

As Cindy would say "Whether you are a fan of dad or not, you bought my book."

So thank you and "2daloo"

ABOUT THE AUTHOR

Born and raised in the hockey world, Cindy gives her perspective on what it was like to have Don Cherry as her father. She observed and learned from his lifestyle and put these lessons toward her own life. From her love of animals, which brought on careers as a vet tech, zookeeper, racetrack groomer, and pet store manager, to owning Canada's first mobile dog-grooming service, she learned to have that entrepreneurial spirit.

She has worked for the Kidney Foundation of Canada as a fund development and marketing associate, an organization close to her heart since donating a kidney to her brother in 1978. The charity work continues within the Cherry family by establishing a facility in honour of her late mother that administers palliative and respite care to chronically ill children. Plus, her love for animals and being an animal-welfare activist prompted her to start Don Cherry's Pet Rescue Foundation, which benefits from the sale of this book.

Cindy hopes you enjoy reading about her Dad's inimitable life as much as she enjoyed sharing it.

Manufactured by Amazon.ca
Bolton, ON

44988536R00122